Alex Taek-Gwang Lee

MADE IN NOWHERE

Essays on the Asiatic Modes of Existence

Made in Nowhere

First Published by Sublation Media 2025
Copyright © 2025 Alex Taek-Gwang Lee

All Rights Reserved
Commissioned and Edited by Douglas Lain
Copy Editor: Konrad Jandavs

A Sublation Press Book
Published by Sublation Media LLC

Distributed by Ingramspark

www.sublationmedia.com

Print ISBN: 979-8-9988244-0-1
eBook ISBN: 979-8-9901591-8-1

Edited and typeset by Polifolia in Germany

Contents

Acknowledgements	vii
Introduction	ix
1. Capitalism in Asia	1
The Ontology of Commodity	3
Questions concerning the Asiatic Mode of Production	7
2. The Political Economy of Global Mobility	12
Leviathan as an Enterprise	14
The Urban "Supermodernity"	17
Tourists and Multitude	22
The Militant Against the Urstaat	25
3. The Viral Interpellation	30
Global Capitalism and Pandemic	33
High Technology and Primitive Exploitation	35
4. Zombie and Demos	38
5. BTS and the Nation-State	43
6. The Desire of *Squid Game*	53
7. The Flesh of Democracy	58
The Ideology of Plastic Surgery	61
Biopolitics in Asia	67
The Failure of Law	73
8. Hegel and Netflix	76
Algorithm and Choice	78
Teleology vs Mechanism	81
Resistance within Mechanisms	83
9. Street Artists in Delhi	86
10. Sartre in Asia	91
The National Question	93
Refugee Ontology	96

11. Foucault and Iran   103
    Politics and Spirituality   105
    Against "Westoxification"   110
    Islamic Heideggerianism   112
    God and Disjunction   114

12. North Korea and the Enigma of Survival   120
    The Democratic Paradox   122
    The Monstrosity of North Korea   127
    The North Korean Lesson   131

13. On the Return of *Top Gun*   136

Postscript: *View of Delft*   143

Endnotes   149

The question is, can mankind fulfil its destiny without a fundamental revolution in the social state of Asia?
—Karl Marx

When this rollback takes place, we must have our own cultural values. And yet perhaps these values do not already exist, in substantive form. Rather I suspect that they are possible as method, that is to say, as the process of the subject's self-formation (*shutai keisei no katei*). This I have called "Asia as method," and yet it is impossible to definitively state what this might mean.
—Takeuchi Yoshimi

Acknowledgements

This book is the outcome of long conversations with my friends. Many parts of this work owe much to Slavoj Žižek, who visited Seoul every summer from 2012 to 2020, during which time I enjoyed regular discussions with him over lunch at a *bibimbap* restaurant. Thanks to Sebastian Hsien-Hao Liao's great arrangement, I had the opportunity to visit National Taiwan University to share my ideas with Taiwanese scholars. My mates in Taiwan, Hung-chiung Li, Chun-Mei Chuang, and Iping Liang, helped me survive in Taipei. Lulu Reyes, Oscar V. Campomanes, and Vincenz Serrano in the Philippines also opened my eyes to the South Sea and the islands. In Japan, Toshiya Ueno is my master who revealed the archipelagic imagination, Azuma Hiroki kindly invited me to contribute to *Genron*, where I could develop my early ideas of capitalism in Asia, and Hitomi Koyama stimulated my understanding of international relations. I must also express my sincere gratitude to Alfie Bown, whose interest in my works encouraged me to make this book.

Introduction

Lu Xun, one of modern China's most notable writers, once stated that Chinese people did not know the meaning of a century before the twentieth century. This does not imply that Chinese people were uncivilized or ill-bred prior to the twentieth century, only that they had a worldview different from the one framed by Judeo-Christian periodization, which shaped the European one. In the preface to his *L'Orphelin de la Chine*, a drama published in 1753 that is a variation of the thirteenth-century Chinese tragedy *l'Orphelin de Tchao*, Voltaire praised the Chinese dramatic achievement for its superiority to European theater. He did not hesitate to call this classical drama a masterpiece in comparison to any French work of the same period. However, his review of traditional Chinese art ended with a critical emphasis on its gridlock. For him, the development of Chinese art had stopped in its infancy, while the European cultures had successfully continued to expand their artistic attainment. Voltaire's judgment of the Chinese and other "Asiatics" of his time aligns with Leibniz's understanding of the unknown country, even though their attitudes toward Christianity were starkly different.

Leibniz observed that "no matter how foolish and paradoxical the Chinese ordinarily appear to be in *re medica*, nevertheless, theirs is better than ours."[1] For him, China was a more advanced civilization than Europe, and the Chinese knowledge of medicine consolidated his conviction. His discovery of China led Leibniz to the "Middle Kingdom" hypothesis, i.e., positing a destined harmony between the kingdom of nature and the kingdom of

God. For Leibniz, the existence of China proved such a pre-established harmony. Unbeknownst to the Chinese, God had prepared the final goal of all civilizations. Leibniz's apprehension of Jesuit missionary letters and books reveals that he regarded China as a different world that did not follow Christian-European rule. This recognition of difference led him to learn of "the Jesuit system of slow penetration into China through a sympathetic understanding of Chinese problems" that employed the gradual introduction of Western scientific methods and religion.[2]

Contrary to Leibniz, Voltaire grasped China and Europe as geographically and culturally distinct entities that nevertheless belonged to the same one world. For him, China is part of worldly multiplicity and is a competitor to Europe. While Leibniz's vision assumed the accomplishment of Christendom for the establishment of harmony, Voltaire believed in historical progress and scientific knowledge. From this perspective, he regarded the Chinese as "the example of a nation that is believed to be the wisest and the best governed in the world."[3] Interestingly, Leibniz and Voltaire both expressed admiration for Chinese medicine as a leading scientific achievement, but they were convinced that Christian Europe was superior to the country. The undeniable presence of China had to be concerned only with God's plan of Christianity. The geographical difference was supposed to be erased by the development of European civilization.

Leibniz's concept of a monad seems to consolidate this faith. For Leibniz, a monad is the essential uniformity of an utterly distinct substance. He argued that "these monads do not make up a whole that is truly one, and the whole, were they to make one up, would not be a mind."[4] More importantly, Leibniz considered matter not a substance but "a *shadow* and even a *nothing*."[5] An army or a flock is a matter, which is "a thing whose *unity* is constructed by our conception."[6] In this sense, matter as the totality of monads is not a substance but, at best, a substantiatum. His understanding of the Dutch East India Company (i.e., the aggregate of monads) is based on this presupposition. Leibniz pointed out that "if parts fitting together in the same plan are more suitable for composing a true substance than those touching, then all the officers of the Dutch East India Company will make up a real substance, far better than a heap of stones."[7] However, the common plan is nothing but a resemblance—"an order of actions and passions that our mind notices in different things."[8] For Leibniz, these assemblages are not an object but merely "fiction of the mind."[9]

Leibniz's approach to the Dutch East India Company, Vereenigde Oostindische Compagnie (VOC) in Dutch, lingers in the West's understanding of Asia to this day. Ironically, the fundamental doctrine of Leibniz's monadology was shared by Voltaire's comprehension of Chinese art, even though the latter's pessimism was not compatible with the former's optimism. Still, both agreed with the proposition that the law of nature rules the world. From this perspective, Leibniz could insist that the Dutch East India Company, the primitive formulation of capitalism, was not an objective substance but a subjective fiction. This early-modern philosophy persists in nearly every discussion of the relationship between Asia and capitalism; most simply see Asia through Leibniz's concept of a monad. Is it true that Asia does not exist as an object? Of course not. Nobody could say that the geographical sense of Asia does not exist today. Yet the problem of explaining Asia-as-object remains. Against Leibniz's argument, Graham Harman suggests an ontological interpretation of the first multinational joint-stock company. The early-modern corporate model of the integrated global supply chain transformed Asia fundamentally at the same time that Leibniz and Voltaire discovered China.

Indeed, the VOC became an authority that claimed to have invented (or reinvented) "Asia" under the rule of capitalist exchange when it began to control the Spice Islands. Like Robinson Crusoe, the company projected the law of capitalism onto these richly interconnected landmasses as if they were desert islands. The Spice Islands were framed as a no-man's-land absorbed into the VOC and bestowed by it with an identity. In this sense, the birth of the VOC is linked to the creation of Asia. Before the VOC's arrival, people in this region did not call themselves "Asians." As Harman clarifies, "The VOC is not the VOC because it conquers the Spice Islands, but conquers the Spice Islands because it is the VOC."[10] Contrary to Leibniz's assumption, the VOC was not "a nicknamed pseudo-substance" but "a pre-existent entity conceptualized as a monopoly within the Netherlands, then at the expense of other European powers, and finally extended to trade within Asia itself."[11] This premise leads us to rethink the modern presence of Asia. Asians did not know that they were Asian when the VOC began its conquests and operations in the region. So-called Asia was a designation that arrived by the hand of the VOC. This recognition does not mean that Asia is a pseudosubstance or European fiction but that it is instead an object, a real assemblage of capitalism.

From this perspective, we must apprehend Lu Xun's statement about China's twentieth century by recounting these conjunctures between Asia and the primordial capitalist accumulation. However, many arguments have quickly fallen into denial of real Asia. For instance, some Western critics have tried, by observing the Confucian culture in Asia, to explain why early control of the COVID-19 pandemic in countries such as China, Taiwan, and South Korea was successful. Confucianism cannot provide us with ontological evidence of the land. Those preconceptions are rooted in a misunderstanding of how Asia served as an object. The Dutch East India Company, as the machine of capitalist accumulation, brought forth the real foundation of Asia. Once established as an object by the capitalist assemblages, Asia was able to be one. Kakuzō Okakura's announcement, i.e., "Asia is one," dramatically approved the accidental birth of a single Asia.[12]

In *The Ideals of the East*, Okakura argued that "the Himalayas divide, only to accentuate, two mighty civilizations, the Chinese with its communism of Confucius, and the Indian with its individualism of the Vedas," yet "not even the snowy barriers can interrupt for one moment that broad expanse of love for the Ultimate and Universal."[13] Here, Okakura emphasized the unity of Asia against geographical division. What is this oneness of Asia? Confucianism or Hinduism does not bring out its wholeness, and One Asia possibly comes to exist beyond geographical differences. Undoubtedly, Asia gained its presence through capitalism, and the VOC substantiated Asia as an object. Capitalism is the establishing force of Asia, which integrates different ethnic groups in the region. In other words, Asia does not have a single identity, and Asians do not stand for a race. One Asia is shaped on the level of a sheer abstraction, i.e., capitalism. Asia will therefore lose its wholeness without the capitalist mode of production. Capitalism in Asia is not particular but universal—"Asian" capitalism is not a premature or underdeveloped economic system. Rather, capitalism in Asia is the most naked revelation of capitalist realism.

Wang Hui, one of the most influential intellectuals in China, also points out that the continuity of premodern China cannot understand China as it is today.[14] The Chinese Revolution in 1911 marks a definitive break between the old China and the new. He regards the Xinhai Revolution as the beginning of "the awakening of Asia" and defines the years between 1911 and 1976 as "China's short twentieth century" that marks the long Chinese revolution. His conception of China's short twentieth century is a counter-discourse to Eric Hobsbawm's periodization. In *Age of Extremes*, Eric Hobsbawm proposed the term "the short twentieth century" to describe the century's extreme experiences. Hobsbawm's designation refers to the 78 years from 1914 to 1991, commencing with World War I and ending with the collapse of the Soviet Union.[15] Wang intends to rewrite the Eurocentric historiography of modernity. He aims to bring forth an alternative perspective to the normative approach to China and is more likely to reveal another layer hidden in Leibniz's and Voltaire's understanding of China under the Christian axiomatics.

However, the problem with Wang's argument is that he sees China as being representative of Asia, while it was historically a part of Asia, not all of it. The Chinese Revolution was not an internal Chinese event but a product of anti-imperialist struggle across Asia. In this sense, China's twentieth century cannot be distinguished from the rest of Asia's twentieth century, not least because the reformist merchants in the South Sea and the revolutionary intellectuals in Japan and Korea enabled the Chinese Revolution. On March 16, 1885, Fukuzawa Yukichi, a Japanese writer and educator, published an article titled "On Leaving Asia" anonymously in the *Jiji shinpō* newspaper. Fukuzawa's piece was a response to the assassination of Kim Ok-gyun, a Korean reformist, by the Korean government, and the article revealed his political disappointment. In the short essay, the Japanese writer insisted that "once the wind of Western civilization blows to the East, every blade of grass and every tree in the East follow what the Western wind brings."[16] Fukuzawa's perception was not far from that of Leibniz and Voltaire, only from a reversed position that regarded the West as a rival to the East. His thought relied on the principle that "civilization ultimately means the progress of man's knowledge and virtue."[17] This belief led him to see Western civilization and enlightenment as the natural law.

From this perspective, Fukuzawa diagnosed China and Korea as ugly adjacent countries that hindered the improvement of Japan's reputation in the world, and he concluded that "these two countries cannot survive as independent nations with the onslaught of Western civilization to the East."[18] In his view, the only way to save these two neighbors from their incompetence was a massive reform effort that would change their governments and transform the spirit of their people, but Fukuzawa believed it unlikely that such a transformation would ever happen. The early-modern Japanese intellectual's analysis ended with a Fichtean plea to the Japanese people: Japan should leave "the ranks of Asian nations and cast [its] lot with civilized nations of the West." [19] Fukuzawa's notion of "leaving Asia" did not mean Asia must be westernized or become another West. Instead, his address urged Japan to be a leader in order to reinvent Asia by abolishing the feudalistic regimes in other Asian countries. This idea of "leaving Asia" was the foundation of Pan-Asianism. For this reason, Fukuzawa and other Japanese reformists such as Oi Kentaro and Miyazaki Toten, supported the republican revolutions in China and Japan.

Despite its logical paradox, i.e., the contradictory motives and tactics for defeating the West via pro-Western chauvinism, their theory of Japanese leadership for Asia gained immense attention among Chinese, Korean, and Filipino revolutionaries. The Japanese advocates of Western learning were "nationalistic enough to believe that Japan, even in its present condition, was sufficiently ahead of the rest of Asia to be able to offer it all that was needed to equal the West."[20] More importantly, the influence of Pan-Asianism did not remain within the boundaries of North-East Asia. For instance, Filipino Asianist thinkers in the nineteenth century saw Japan as "a potential ally, protector, and Asian power with which to be associated in their anti-colonial struggle."[21] The radical legacy of Pan-Asianism resonated with both the Communist International in the colonial period and the Non-Aligned Movement during the Cold War era. This ideological backdrop paved the way for the Philippine Revolution in 1895 before the Chinese Revolution. To be sure, China's twentieth century is part of the long revolution in Asia, which cannot be reduced to the order of the nation-states. As Wang admits, China has never been a nation-state but has instead participated in the birth of Asia as an object. In other words, Asia is not Leibniz's sense of "shadow" or "nothing" but the light of an object, i.e., the absence of darkness. As Fukuzawa implied, the doctrine of modern Asia was not Confucianism but Faustian technology.

In 1919, shortly after World War I, Paul Valéry wrote an open letter, "The Crisis of the Mind," about the disillusionment of European civilization. He declared, "She felt in every nucleus of her mind that she was no longer the same, that she was no longer herself, that she was about to lose consciousness, a consciousness acquired through centuries of bearable calamities, by thousands of men of the first rank, from innumerable geographical, ethnic, and historical coincidences."[22] However, he also emphasized the possibility for a rebirth of Europe's soul more vigorous than before if the right decisions were made in the face of this crisis. Twelve years after Valéry's letter, Oswald Spengler published a little book, *Man and Technics*, when another world war was approaching. In his consideration of technics as the European legacy, he argued that "instead of keeping strictly to itself the technical knowledge that constituted their greatest asset, the 'white' peoples complacently offered it to all the world" and that the Japanese then "became technicians of the first rank, and in their war against Russia they revealed a technical superiority from which their teachers were able to learn many lessons."[23]

For Spengler, the crisis of European civilization resulted from the universalization of technology and, consequently, the beginning of "the exploited world's revenge on its masters." Like Valéry, his solution to this decline of Europe, i.e., "the Faustian civilization," was the revival of "a *spiritual* need" rather than the Faustian technics—"not its economic consequence, but its *victories*."[24] He criticized "machine technology," which would quickly approach a dead end, and against this universal unification of technology he insisted that Europeans instead pursue "a short life, full of deeds and glory" rather than "a long and empty one." The thoughts of Valéry and Spengler on the European crisis concerning technological globalization, mainly accelerated by technological diffusion and the spread of technology across borders, mirrored Fukuzawa's acclaim of technological universalism. In this sense, Asia was the double image of the West brought up by the lightness of the Faustian civilization.

In this collection of essays, I attempt to bring forth the substantial foundation of Asia. This does not mean that I would like to set out a solid framework with which to pin down the elusive identity of Asia. Asia is the loci where capitalist production has since its genesis gained the necessary resources for its accumulation, and capitalism is the substantial uniformity of Asia. In this vein, I regard the problem of Asia as the universal question of capitalism. The scope of this book is varied but focuses on how the area functions as the cogwheels of global capitalism. Each essay engages topics ranging from the COVID-19 pandemic to BTS, a Korean pop music boy band, via a Delhi protest, the Iranian Revolution, Netflix, the beauty industry, and zombies. I hope these analyses will be a valuable theoretical intervention in the established scholarship of Asian Studies beyond postcolonialism.

1.
Capitalism in Asia

SINCE THE FINANCIAL CRISIS OF 2008, we have witnessed astounding proclamations indicating that capitalism is dead or at least dying. A similar scene repeated amid the COVID-19 pandemic. Some experts quickly anticipated the end of global capitalism and the onset of a new cold war. The emergence from the left of rhetorical expressions such as these was not surprising; however, in this case, the subjects of these utterances were interesting enough. They were not the left but those who had stood in opposition to the leftist demand to end capitalism. Politicians, policymakers, people in business, as well as liberal economists and even comedians all seemed to be waiting for capitalism's last breath. However, capitalism did not die. It has survived, and so we still live in a world of ridiculous "transformers."

Why is this happening? How does capitalism sustain itself? Many arguments attempt to explain capitalism's survival, but I think this is the point where we should return to Marx's analysis of capitalism and his approach to the secret of capital, so to speak, which is the problem of the commodity. We need to reconsider the enigmatic relationship between commodities and capitalism. The material foundation of global capitalism resides in the multinational division of labor and the worldwide distribution of commodities. In this capitalist logistics, Asian countries have played a crucial role since World War II. The Cold War was a geopolitical strategy to invent so-called Asia. For most of the people in Asia, the Cold War was not so much "cold" as the "hottest" warfare.

After the collapse of the socialist bloc, Asian countries seemed to be turned into a "Factory Asia" based on regional supply chains and cheap labor power in the global economy. Asia was once the revolutionary countries of a red flag, but it now became the land of promise for global capitalism. Global task allocation allowed China to become the central hub of the Global Value Chain (GVC) and at the same time accelerated the integration of trade and the disintegration of production. This global transformation resulted in a separation between consumption and production, which seemed to undermine the role of nation-states in international relations. As Zygmunt Bauman argues, this retreat of the nation-state means that state power is increasingly seen as only being administrative and less and less often being the governance of national passion.[1]

It is undeniable that the survival of capitalism since the crisis of 2008 lies with the Asian supply chain, which remained undiminished by the financial collapse. However, the analysis seems to lack due consideration of the fact that Asia is not only the factory but also a market based on telecommunication technology such as the Internet. This technology-based market forges the unconscious level of global capitalism and the cultural logic of commodities. The commodities are not simple objects, instead representing specific values which have a hidden layer of their existence. The values of any commodity depend on the accidental relations of exchange and come to erase their origins. As Slavoj Žižek points out, the secret of a commodity lies in its form like the Freudian sense of "dream-work." By analyzing Marx's brilliant concept of commodity fetishism, Žižek states that "in the commodity-form, there is definitely more at stake than the commodity-form itself, and it was precisely this 'more' which exerted such a fascinating power of attraction."[2] Here, Žižek clarifies the latent link between Marx and psychoanalysis, which reveals the unconscious level of commodification, the fetishism of the commodity-form.

However, his analysis must be pushed forward to the ontological level of a commodity if we want to understand the full mechanism of commodification.

The Ontology of Commodity

I would like to introduce my personal experience regarding this matter. It happened when I visited Chinatown in Kuala Lumpur, the capital of Malaysia. As I elbowed my way through the crowd, some vendors solicited me with their counterfeit luxury watches. I ignored them, but one of the sellers clasped my sleeve and insisted, "This is a fake, but the same as the original one." An idea occurred to me at that moment: if there is no difference between the imitation and the original, how can we demarcate luxury goods from the non-luxury ones? What is the meaning of luxury without such a distinction? Furthermore, what makes the luxury commodity a luxury commodity in itself? These could be considered questions about the ontology of the commodity.

Another episode I witnessed in my country, South Korea, can clarify these issues. In 2010, according to a newspaper, South Korean police arrested a man who produced and sold knock-off luxury bags from brands such as Chanel, Louis Vuitton, Gucci, Prada, etc. More interestingly, the report said that the man had once worked as an equipment manufacturer for such luxury companies, making luxury imitations for 22 years after he quit the job. Thus, it seemed not at all strange when the suspect insisted that he must be called a craftsman and not merely a criminal.

These are not simply jokes about luxury production and consumption but instead reveal a truth about capitalism, in particular, the structure of commodities. The incidents I described above explain what justifies a commodity as a commodity. In light of the occasions in question, not every commodity is permitted to exist as an authentic commodity, although a fake commodity has its own value in the market. The criterion that determines which one is an authentic commodity and which one isn't is significant to register the logic of commodity fetishism. What is the measure that registers a commodity as authentic? The value of a commodity is defined by something else, something which is not itself included in that commodity. A commodity is not autonomous but always already related to another dimension, i.e., the relation of exchange. In this sense, Marx's definition of commodification can reveal the problem of commoditization in general.

For Marx, the commodity is the secret to capitalist dynamics. To understand the dynamic system of capitalism, he analyzes the movement of capital as "a process of value expansion or wealth augmentation."[3] There is a circulation of commodities at the core of the vigorous enlargement of capitalist fortune. This is the reason Marx begins his famous inquiry of capital with the dissection of commodities. The dissemination of commodities means the formation of prices, i.e., the exchange of a commodity for money and money for another commodity. The general formula for the mechanism wherein commodities are transformed into money, which is then transformed back into commodities, is C-M-C; this explains how the accumulation of capital happens. The exchange process produces the values of commodities; thus, the form of a commodity is open to the relations between sellers and buyers. The circulation of commodities that subsist under such relations could be called a market.

A commodity is in this respect the product of social relations. No individual could produce a commodity. He or she can make a product through his or her labor but cannot produce a commodity. A commodity requires social production and exchange while interceding the division of labor and expediting the reproduction of another commodity. In this way, the sale of commodities is partly used for more commodity production in a cycle that replenishes such production. However, as Marx points out, the capitalist diffusion of commodities is not merely the exchange of products as it occurs during bartering, since the former exchange is always mediated by money. The notion of monetized prices is the crucial hub for the wheel of commodities. As Marx argues,

> Even if an individual article, or a definite quantity of one kind of commodity, may contain simply the social labour required to produce it, and as far as this aspect is concerned the market value of this commodity represents no more than the necessary labour, yet, if the commodity in question is produced on a scale that exceeds the social need at the time, a part of the society's labour-time is wasted, and the mass of commodities in question then represents on the market a much smaller quantity of social labour than it actually contains … These commodities must therefore be got rid of at less than their market value, and a portion of them may even be completely unsalable … But if the volume of social labour spent on the production of a certain article corresponds in scale to the social need to be satisfied, so that the amount produced corresponds to the customary measure of reproduction, given an unchanged demand, then the commodity will be sold at its market value. The exchange or sale of commodities at their value is the rational, natural law of the equilibrium between them; not the converse, i.e. the law of equilibrium should not be derived from contemplating the divergence.[4]

Marx suggests that reproduction prices are relative. The assessment of commodities depends on their relationship to another commodity. In this sense, the truth of the prices lies in the actual exchange of commodities rather than the natural law of the equilibrium. The prices could be changed by a transformation in the reproduction of commodities or the magnitudes of values. For Marx, values are the complicated determinant of the reproduction price. The reproduction price is not related to labor productivity but instead revolves around the values. How are the values determined? A theologian like Saint Thomas Aquinas would argue that only God could define the values. What about today? Is Aquinas's presupposition still useful for understanding the relationship between prices and values in capitalism? What Aquinas meant by God was the norm of natural law. With the advent of capitalism, the heavenly rule was changed, being replaced with the more secular version, i.e., the market of *homo economicus*. However, the category of natural law is still working. What is considered the natural law for values now?

For Aquinas, natural law is the rational capacity to participate in the eternal law and the guidance and measure of human acts. Conversely, natural law could be a rationale to justify the determinants of values. It is not difficult to see this reversed phenomenon in capitalist society. Marx's analysis of commodity fetishism is firmly grounded in the circumstance of commodification. Money is used as the norm for prices in the commodifying effect. Different from values, the determinants of prices rest on the exchange of commodities, not the values produced by labor. Abiding by this criterion, producers calculate prices to sustain the reproduction of commodities. To reproduce commodities, material resources and labor time are necessarily required. In this way, "assessing the quantity of resources required to produce a commodity in economies characterized by a division of labor is in effect assessing the amount of direct and indirect labor time required to produce it."[5] This proves the correctness of Marx's presumption that reproduction prices must be set on the basis of values.

Here, I don't wish to discuss further Marx's analysis of the connection between prices and values and his preoccupation with transforming the value of inputs into the prices of production. Suffice it to say that the prices of commodities cannot help but reflect values. This difference is important. According to Marx's discovery, there is a discrepancy between prices and values, and the confusing of these categories resides in commodity fetishism. This is the reason why such an effect gyrates around all commodities. As is well known, Marx's conceptualization of fetishism is an attempt to understand the effect of the commodity form in producing a formal equality. The problem of the commodity form is the fetishism of equal exchange by which everything is simply transformed into an equalized value in the abstract regardless of substantive differences in use value.

Questions concerning the Asiatic Mode of Production

It is György Lukács who formulated the theory of reification from Marx's discussion of commodity fetishism and defined its essential aspect as the ghostly objectivity of commodity form. For Lukács, it is reification that obstructs epistemological totalization in capitalist society, specifically the rationalization of a world operated by commodity-structure. This process of rational objectification subsequently conceals the immediate qualitative and material character of things as things. This is the very process of reification through capitalist rationalization; rationalization transforms any quality of natural materials into the symbolically quantitative dimension. Marx also analyzes this symbolizing mechanism of rationalization when explaining the relation between time and the clock—"the clock was the first automatic device applied to practical purpose; the whole theory of the production of regular motion was developed through it."[6]

As Charlie Chaplin's film *Modern Times* clearly manifests, the clock is an ideological apparatus, so to speak, whereby the rationalization of capitalism comes to occupy human consciousness as well as the unconscious. When Lukács conceptualizes the meaning of reification, it refers not only to the rationalization of human relationships in a capitalist society but also to the individual and collective psychological effect generated by the process of the symbolic mechanism. It is in this sense that reification can be seen as a matrix in which the chemistry of ideological production is closely linked to individual fantasy. This is where a question arises as to how such a psychological effect is verified by commodity-structure. Commodities in and of themselves cannot control or influence our minds. Commodities have no power in this regard. Marx points this out clearly when he writes,

> Commodities cannot themselves go to market and perform exchanges in their own right. We must, therefore, have recourse to their guardians, who are the possessors of commodities. Commodities are things, and therefore lack the power to resist man. If they are unwilling, he can use force; in other words, he can take possession of them. In order that these objects may enter into relation with each other as commodities, their guardians must place themselves in relation to one another as persons whose will resides in those objects, and must behave in such a way that each does not appropriate the commodity of the other, and alienate his own, except through an act to which both parties consent. The guardians must therefore recognize each other as owners of private property. This juridical relation, whose form is the contract, whether as part of a developed legal system or not, is a relation between two wills which mirrors the economic relation. The content of this juridical relation (or relation of two wills) is itself determined by the economic relation. Here the

persons exist for one another merely as representatives and hence owners, of commodities.[7]

What should be stressed in Marx's argument is that the juridical relation is nothing less than the economic relationship embedded in private property. In this respect, the economic association cannot be separated from the juridical relation. That is to say, commodities are always embedded in a legal system that protects their owners' interests. The natural ontology of commodities—in other words, the naturalizing structure of commodification—goes hand in hand with legalization. Evgeny Pashukanis, one of the leading authorities on Soviet legal science, provides a useful analysis with which we can understand the naturalization of capitalism through the commodity structure. As he argues, "Property becomes the basis of the legal form only when it becomes something which can be freely disposed of in the market."[8] The circulation of commodities is the condition through which the juridical relation comes to exist, because only a freeman, i.e., a proletarian and not a slave, can own and sell his or her commodities such as labor power. As Pashukanis says, the freeman is trapped in the legal system, treated as an object and subject to "the same prohibitions and quota allocations under the immigration laws as are other commodities imported across national boundaries."[9]

For this reason, the individual worker in capitalist society becomes a legal subject and a bearer of rights whereas the product of labor transforms into a commodity and a bearer of value. This procedure succeeds in simultaneously naturalizing both capitalism and commodification as normative frameworks. The real subsumption of legalization transforms a worker into a consumer, while the formal subsumption of commodification forges a worker from a peasant. Returning to the episodes I introduced at the beginning of this text, it is the juridical judgment that declares which one is an authentic commodity and which one is not.

Furthermore, there is a legal subject, a bearer of rights, that acquires the capacity to be "human capital" under the so-called new spirit of capitalism.

It is critical to account for the interaction between legalization and commodification in order to revitalize Marx's analysis of the commodity form concerning fetishism today. According to Pierre Dardot and Christian Laval, liberal interventionism since the 1950s has aimed "to restore the conditions for free competition ... in order to ensure the 'victory of the fittest'" by focusing on legal justifications and equal treatment before law.[10] The recent tendency of liberal interventionism has been to provide the grounds for an administrative state, which might be necessary to defend the juridical justice of free competition. It is not an exaggeration to say that the transmutation of liberalism is related to the incorporation of a legal subject, the abstract will of the commodity owner, and capitalism. The tacit compliance of the subject with such normative legislation could be one of the sustaining factors in the survival of capitalism and its transformation of the human condition. Asia, as a global factory and market, has played a crucial role in building up these new norms of capitalism. Asian capitalism is no longer at the margins of globalization but is now the very essence of it.

In *A Contribution to the Critique of Political Economy*, Marx wrote that "in broad lines Asiatic, ancient, feudal, and modern bourgeois modes of production can be designated as progressive epochs in the economic formation of society."[11] Here, Marx listed the Asiatic mode as one of the various modes of production, and his conceptualization of it seems to warrant the reconsideration of Marx's approach to Asia. Even though Edward Said criticized Marx for being a European who was not free from Orientalism, a letter from Marx to Vera Zasulich in 1881 proves that Marx himself recognized the alternative to the European mode of production. He wrote that his discussion of the "historical inevitability" of the primitive accumulation movement is expressly limited to the countries of Western Europe.[12] Marx's view on the multi-lineality of the social transition leads us to rethink Asian capitalism alongside his early definition of the Asiatic mode of production. Asia would be the perfect locus from which to revive Marx with a new critique of political economy.

2.

The Political Economy of Global Mobility

THE MOVEMENT OF PEOPLE AND GOODS is the material foundation of global capitalism. The high degree of mobility enabled by developed transportation such as air travel has accelerated globalization. Whoever encounters the reality of the terrestrial integration should consider the effects of global mobility on each local identity. Primitive accumulation in capitalism would be impossible if there were no geographical difference. It all began with trade but ended up with imperialism and colonization. Karl Marx was one of the nineteenth-century European intellectuals who was preoccupied with this early form of globalization. Observing the first stage of global capitalism, Marx pointed out that "the discovery of gold and silver in America, the extirpation, enslavement and entombment in mines of the indigenous population of that continent, the beginnings of the conquest and plunder of India, and the conversion of Africa into a preserve for the commercial hunting of blackskins, are all things which characterize the dawn of the era of capitalist production."[1] Following this early stage of accumulation, the globe becomes the battlefield of the European empires' commercial war.

As Marx describes, imperial expansion is nothing less than the creation of the world in the image of the European bourgeoisie. This imperialism did not bring forth a unified world but instead belied colonial subsumption and racialized differentiation. Capitalist expansion in the twentieth century resulted in two destructive wars and the rise of nation-states in its aftermath. Postwar nation-states are simultaneously the political venue of decolonization and another battleground for socialism and capitalism. However, following the collapse of the socialist bloc in the 1990s, the nation-state came to play a role different from that of its political origins. The nation-state as the material realization of a nation, i.e., an imagined community, shifts to become the promoter of globalization. The tension here between nationalization and globalization seems to have waned, but it remains unresolved. From the ruins of empire, this globalist project first substitutes for colonialism and then after the 1980s comes to be known more commonly as neoliberalism. Despite the many criticisms of what is called neoliberalism, its champions believe that the global system, the economic replacement of old empire, is a regulated world in which capital and goods move freely according to the principle of supply and demand, producing prosperity for all.

In this sense, the novel dimension of today's global mobility lies with the logistics of people and goods within and beyond national governmentality. These logistical flows construct local and global supply chains comprising infrastructure, people, goods, and information. In her book about global logistics, Deborah Cowen argues:

> Casually referred to by those in the industry as a "pipeline," logistics space contrasts powerfully with the territoriality of the national state. Today, the supply chain is understood to be both vital and vulnerable and so in urgent need of protection. This networked space surfaces over and over again as the object of supply chain security, rendering its trademark cartography. The corporate supply chain has a history in the military and colonial supply line. It is no accident that the supply chain of contemporary capitalism resonates so clearly with the supply line of the colonial frontier.[2]

What must be stressed here is the new role of nation-states in the rise of globalizing logistics. Under the neoliberal model, each nation-state takes on a crucial role in creating markets. The neoliberal government of the state is the dramatic transformation of the state-machine, i.e., the Leviathan, whose body comprises all the bodies of its citizens. When Thomas Hobbes uses the metaphor to describe the unity of the commonwealth between the sovereign and the people, he presupposes the people's authorization of a common representative to act in their names. According to Hobbes, the state is one person as the representative of the sovereign authority, but not the representation of itself. The state must incorporate each single constituent member, for it is the *unity* of the "representer," not the "represented," that makes the representer "*one.*"[3] This argument tacitly reveals the paradox of the state: the sovereign power as one person must exist prior to the representation of the people and bring forth its capacity to act as one. In other words, the one person held up by the united multitude as a common representative is also created by the sovereign.

Leviathan as an Enterprise

Indeed, it is the sovereign who decides which people can be included or excluded from representation. The logic of the modern state operates as if the commonwealth squarely corresponds with the representation of all members. Still, the unity of the "representer" has already been established before its representative embodiment. In this sense, the body of any democratic polity always already preserves the exceptional state of sovereignty. Therefore, neoliberal globalization does not abolish the hidden impetus behind the modern state but instead reinforces its capability to unite people as one by the exclusion of those who are not to be included in the unity. This enhancement of the authority leads to the modification of the role of nation-states in building up the global supply chain of commodities. With this novel role, the Leviathan becomes an enterprise to administrate economic policy and markets. There is no retreat of the state here but instead the reassertion of the sovereignty as one person. The local governments of nation-states universalize competition and create market-oriented systems of action for individuals, business groups and institutions. The new task of regional administration fundamentally reshapes the utopian credo of a nation-state, i.e., the equality of all members within its communal boundary.

A nation-state is the material foundation of a nation. The imagined nation is rooted in the idea of the commonwealth, and in the republican ideal, in particular. Based on the republican constitution, the nation-state mostly aims to protect property but at the same time presupposes absolute equality among the members of the nation. Two aspects of the nation-state are consolidated in the ideology of national prosperity. In the process of nation-building, this ideology works in tandem with sovereign power to shape the multitude into the unified concept of a people. Michel Foucault points out the primitive violence required in the birth of a nation, since the disciplinary power of sovereignty, unlike in Hobbes's presupposition, does not mean the end of wars, instead bringing forth another war: the violent decision regarding who within the border of a nation-state is included or excluded.[4] The war within the state is a civil war, the return of *bellum omnium contra omnes*, the war of all against all. This theoretical model for permanent struggle with one another explains the homeostasis of a nation-state. The imaginary of a nation, which arises from the transcendental idea of universal right, i.e., the absolute equality of the national members, always already overdetermines the presence of people and the reality of the nation-state. According to Foucault,

> The individual as such, in his relationship with others, is the bearer of this permanent possibility of the war of all against all. If there is in fact a war of all against all, it is first of all essentially because men are equal in the objects and ends they set their sights on, because they are equivalent in the means they possess for obtaining what they seek. They are, as it were, substitutable for each other, and that is precisely why they seek to replace each other and, when something is offered to the desire of one, the other may always substitute himself for the first, wanting to take his place and appropriate what he desires. This substitutability, this convergence of desire characterizes this original competition.[5]

Foucault calls this principle a "quasi-equality" that preserves the "dimension of distrust." Through this suspicion, each individual in the nation-state knows well that someone else may come to replace them. What must be stressed here is that this dynamic of competition is the most crucial feature to provide the basis for the sovereign. In my opinion, Foucault's insight here regarding state power reveals how the lack of trust brings the war of all against all back into the nation-state. If it did not provide a solution to civil war, the nation-state would not be sustainable, and successful nation-building would then require the overcoming of mutual distrust and the reducing of competition between different groups. The political solution to the problem is to create the glorious person, i.e., a scenario in which "one of these perpetual combatants" will dominate the others through some form of additional power.[6] The power of glory is, of course, the system of signs, the instrumental function of nationalism to bring together those individuals who are at the point of civil war within a nation-state. For this reason, the eruption of civil war indicates the terminal state of the sovereign and the disappearance of their unity.

It seems to me that this Hobbesian fantasy is the foundation that enables nationalism to maintain the ideological rationale of the nation-state. However, the rise of neoliberal globalization threatens the basis for national integrity. Many arguments about this transformation of the nation-state have mainly focused on the neoliberal shift of governmentality from a social welfare system to a market economy. With this shift, governments seem to have necessarily retreated from playing a role in markets. From the perspective of political economy, it is undeniable that global interconnection yields more dynamic interaction. Some common concepts in the age of neoliberal globalization include the stateless corporation, a global financial market that functions around the clock, intense competition under flexible capital and the rule of a single price, and a globally connected information society. However, one of the essential features of this transformation is the ascendance of global urbanism. The upsurge of the global city imposes significant alterations on the *raison d'État* of a nation-state.

The Urban "Supermodernity"

There is a familiar argument that revolves around the relationship between globalization and nation-states and points out the relative weakening of the latter. This point of view mainly focuses on the diminishment of national economies under globalization. As Jan Nederveen Pieterse argues, however, "Globalization can mean the reinforcement of both supranational and subnational regionalism."[7] The theory of postmodernism seeks to carve out a politics of hybridity in the dialectic of globalization and localization. More interestingly, the cultural entanglements do not mean that the nation-state as such comes to be multicultural but instead that it is divided by global urbanization. No doubt, the rapid improvement of mobility via technology and connectivity increasingly precipitates the emergence of global cities and the universalization of urbanism. My argument is that the rise of the cosmopolitan megalopolis among nation-states is the foundation of global mobility. Globalization signifies the disintegration of national and local borders, and the primary cities of each nation-state come to function as an intensively interconnected hub of global logistics.

In this way, global cities no longer belong to the national space but instead become detached and isolated from it. The international metropolis simply serves as the totality of "non-places." As Marc Augé points out, "if a place can be defined as relational, historical and concerned with identity, then a space which cannot be defined as relational, or historical, or concerned with identity will be a non-place."[8] In other words, non-places are the areas without identity, such as "the mobile cabins called 'means of transport' (aircraft, trains and road vehicles), the airports and railway stations, hotel chains, leisure parks, large retail outlets, and finally the complex skein of cable and wireless networks."[9] "Supermodernity," which succeeds Baudelaire's conceptualization of modernity, produces these non-places; "transit points and temporary abodes." However, Augé's concept of supermodernity, the condition of the non-places, needs to be further clarified, since he seems to assume a break between modernity and supermodernity. The latter is an excessive modernity that includes features such as the "overabundance of events, spatial overabundance, [and] the individualization of references."[10]

Yet the "excessive" factors are not only employed in the explanation of supermodernity. The flourishing of non-places is not limited to supermodernity since modernity always already precipitated an overwhelming flow of people and goods. Marx and Engels provided a description of capitalism wherein all that is solid melts into air; the lightness and weightlessness of modernity. In 1848, they had already pointed out that the global extension of the bourgeois market gave rise to modern liquidity; in their words, "The need of a constantly expanding market for its products chases the bourgeoisie over the whole surface of the globe."[11] In this sense, colonialism is the early phase of global capitalism and remains embodied in modernity's cultural logic. I therefore contend that there has been no fundamental break between modernity and supermodernity and that many continuities have been inherited from the early phase of globalization. What is nonetheless different between modernity and supermodernity is the advancement of transportation and communication technology. In particular, the progress of aviation technology and information technology, e.g., the Internet, have rapidly increased global mobility. For this reason, the unprecedented growth of international logistics, prompted by new technology, should be regarded as the material foundation for the non-places.

Non-places are, in this sense, nothing other than the fluidity of urban spatio-temporality and the nodal points of global connectivity. Global urbanism's liquid modality, which removes history and identity from geographical locations, is the de facto bedrock of supermodernity. In Baudelaire's sense, the anonymous crowd is the protagonist of the modern city, but the non-places of the global megalopolis have no leading character. On the surface, cultural hybridity comes to exist in the segregated urban space within a nation-state; yet the deeper layer of spatial experience is essentially homogenous, i.e., a single modality of urban consumerism is dominant in such cosmopolitan multiculturalism. Whatever it takes at the local level, everything must be modified by the global standard's refined demands. Urbanity becomes the daily norms of life embedded in globalization. The "noble savage," an early figure of radical Enlightenment, is replaced with the typical image of the metropolitan elite. Urban cosmopolitanism is a mixed breed not equally enjoyed by all who live in the nation-state. This inequality stands against a political doctrine of nationalism that promises the members of a nation-state absolute equality yet brings the unification of sovereignty and people into crisis. Due to this split between a people and its representatives, democracy does not work and the political catastrophe of the nation-state results in the rise of populism.

What must be stressed here is that urban-centrism brings forth new modes of existence. The city dwellers are not only those who populate urban areas but also the consumers of city commerce. Metropolitan consumerism gains its ultimate form in tourism, the commodification of leisure. As Dean MacCannell argues in his classic analysis of the tourist, the highly commercialized space of global cities can be called "a *stage set*, a *tourist setting*, or simply, a *set* depending on how purposefully worked up for tourists the display is."[12] Daniel Boorstin's description of the tourist as the consumer of a pseudoadventure is one such orthodox example that criticizes the fabricated environment the tourist inhabits.[13] According to Boorstin, the tourist, whose risks are insurable, does not venture to encounter any natives in an unknown place but instead embraces the mirror image of themselves wherever they visit. In this way, intellectuals often criticize the figure of the tourist (as opposed to the adventurer) for being shallow and superficial. They argue that the experiences of the tourist are inauthentic and inherently mystified, even when these experiences present themselves as revelations of truth. However, touristic settings are "not merely copies or replicas of real-life situations but copies that are presented as disclosing more about the real thing than the real thing itself discloses."[14] What Boorstin does not recognize in his criticism of the tourist is that tourism *per se* constitutes a failed resistance to metropolitan elitism, which ultimately gains success in confirming touristic settings.

Meanwhile, MacCannell provides an account of the tourist as the ontological condition of modern man. He claims that tourism is a failed attempt to overcome alienation and that it results in the reaffirmation of alienation. Due to this alienated state of existence, the tourist is always blamed for their superficial understanding of other people and places, i.e., for their lack of objectivity and their inability to see things as they ought to be seen. In MacCannell's sense, global tourism is the expansion of modernity and the alienating obfuscation of the distinction between work and leisure. He argues:

> In industrial society, work is broken down into "occupations" and it provides livelihood and status on the individual level. Modern society transforms this same work into a positive and negative aesthetic of production ... The work displays about to be discussed, and the work displays in general, unify economics and aesthetics and they begin to replace industrial concerns for social class and status with the modern concern for "lifestyle." They dramatize the enormous differentiation of the modern work force and, at the same time, reintegrate all classes of workers, from stock brokers to sewer cleaners, in a single system of representations. They obscure the distinction industrial society makes between human and machine labor by displaying the two as inextricably linked in unified design as occurs, for example, in tours of assembly lines.[15]

The point of his argument is that the real in the work resists the symbolic structure of tourism. The work is what is repressed, i.e., the unconscious layer, in the dramatization and representation of tourism. Even though workers and tourists occupy separate social spaces, the visible presence of labor forces tourists to confront the authentic reality of society, regardless of which attraction they view. MacCannell's theory of the tourist elucidates the structure of tourism and the constancy of the tourist as modern man. Nevertheless, his semiotic analysis of the tourist's attraction to sightseeing underestimates global tourism's political economy, which precipitates the spatial separation of tourist areas from any domestic territory.

Tourists and Multitude

To push MacCannell's idea further, Hiroki Azuma's philosophy of the tourist deserves attention here. For Azuma, the tourist is a philosophical theme for understanding the dialectical relationship between Empire and nation-states and can be defined as a "postal multitude."[16] Drawing on political philosophy and critical theory, he combines two key theoretical frameworks: the concept of the "multitude" developed by Antonio Negri and Michael Hardt in their analysis of global power structures, and Jacques Derrida's philosophical examination of postal systems as networks of communication and meaning. In *Empire*, Negri and Hardt argue that "the creative forces of the multitude that sustain Empire are also capable of autonomously constructing a counter-Empire, an alternative political organization of global flows and exchanges."[17] Azuma critically considers this conceptualization of the multitude and attempts to turn its political weaknesses into strengths. For him, the concept's most fundamental problem resides in the way in which there is no possible political agenda in Negri and Hardt's theory of the multitude.[18] According to him, the multitude's only rationale is the self-organization of global networks. Furthermore, its political motivations and orientations are very ambiguous because they merely suggest that "biopower and communism, cooperation and revolution remain together, in love, simplicity, and also innocence."[19] These virtues, i.e., love, simplicity, and innocence, are ethical rather than political, and Azuma argues that Negri and Hardt's optimistic vision of the multitude as such ironically reveals the political powerlessness of their concept.

On the contrary, Azuma discovers the possibility of the tourist in the political failure of the multitude. For him, the problem of the multitude stems from the fact that it cannot have grand narratives to unify itself under a single political doctrine. The rejection of orthodox political thought is its ontological essence; nevertheless, the absence of traditional utopianism, or the skepticism toward *realpolitik*, is paradoxically the most fragile aspect of the multitude. Indeed, Azuma's concept of the tourist shares the same condition of global capitalism with Negri and Hardt's concept of the multitude; however, his assumption is that a tourist is nothing less than the reification of "misdelivery"(誤配), the incarnation of failed communication that contains many performative possibilities. The tourist comes to exist where the multitude fails to gain its unification. Misdelivery, the delivery of goods to the wrong party, is the tourist's condition, and it leads to an unpredictable situation. What the tourist wants to see is often contradicted by what they actually experience. In this way, travel always pertains to an otherness that the tourist cannot predict and that must be supplemented by posteriority. There is no actual alliance, but the subsequent repetitive configuration of supplements sustains the possibility of the association. This idea is similar to MacCannell's affirmation of the tourist as one who participates in others' lives. The tourist's encounter with others at the places they visit is modern man's existential condition. Both MacCannell and Azuma regard the tourist as the ontological form of high modernity and the generic mode of existence in global capitalism. In this sense, the tourist could be called the embodiment of cosmopolitanism and the European Enlightenment's global realization.

In my view, however, the multitude is not merely the mirror image of the tourist but is the primordial substance of those who suffer from global capitalism. The concept is spun off from Spinoza's monism and aims to explain ontological multiplicity. Therefore, it is not wrong to say that tourists are much the same as the multitude, in that the multitude has various modes of existence. Negri and Hardt clearly describe the "postmodern" prototype of the multitude as the militant. They argue that "as the figure of the people dissolves, the militant is the one who best expresses the life of the multitude: the agent of biopolitical production and resistance against Empire."[20] Their examples of the militant mainly include communist and liberatory combatants, antifascist intellectuals, republicans during the Spanish civil war and resistance movements during World War II, and anticolonial and anti-imperialist guerrilla warriors. Here, Negri and Hardt suggest that the concept of the multitude is counter-Hobbesian; the multitude does not belong to nation-states any longer. This idea corresponds to Marx and Engels's grave-digger dialectic: the capitalist mode of production inevitably produces its destroyer, the proletariat. Negri and Hardt insist that the dialectical movement finally ends with the ossification of the socialist states. Negri and Hardt intend to criticize state socialism with the concept of the multitude. The militant is the figure that has already come to exist through previous resistance within and without the nation-state.

Contra Negri and Hardt's understanding of the multitude, I would suggest that the multitude discloses the paradox of political economy within Empire; the labor force of global capitalism must stay within domestic assembly lines even though it works for global companies, and the only way that local workers can cross the borders of nation-states is as tourists. Any worker, to the extent that they're regarded as part of the labor force, cannot travel across national boundaries. Of course, a tourist is not a militant. Azuma's concept of the tourist sheds light on this ontological distinction between the two modes of existence. I would like to go beyond his argument. My assumption is that the factor that makes a member of the labor force become a particular tourist is the legal right of travel. A tourist must be identified as the legitimate citizen of a nation-state, while a militant resists the authority's national identification. If you need legal permission to visit a country, it means that you are always subsumed by the nation-state. This fact proves that nation-states are not the outside of Empire but are instead the parts of its assemblages. Nationalism, the absent cause of nation-states, consists of the partial drives within Empire; however, it does not ensure the dissolution of the state form. In this sense, it is the ontological mode of the militant, not the tourist, that is the more salient incarnation of the multitude. Ironically, the militant is neither citizen nor tourist but a third mode of existence between nation-state and Empire. It remains in the national territory while being politically dislocated by its global engagement from within. I think that this political disjunction is the critical gap between the tourist and the militant; the tourist is never displaced with the nation-state, while the militant struggles to be dismembered from the national body.

The Militant Against the Urstaat

In this sense, the militant should be understood as one who resists authority to claim their right of travel and who identifies themselves with those who have no such documents, i.e., *sans papiers*. As the primordial substance of the militant, the ontological state of the multitude is closer to that of the refugee than to that of the tourist. According to Negri and Hardt, the multitude is "social flesh" that is not a body but "a flesh that is common, living substance":

> The flesh of multitude is pure potential, an unformed life force, and in this sense an element of social being, aimed constantly at the fullness of life. From this ontological perspective, the flesh of the multitude is an elemental power that continuously expands social being, producing in excess of every traditional political-economic measure of value [...] From the perspective of political order and control, then, the elemental flesh of the multitude is maddeningly elusive, since it cannot be

entirely corralled into the hierarchical organs of a political body.[21]

The flesh of the multitude is the deformation of the Leviathan's body, the expansion of social being against the unification of people and the sovereign, and the excessive production of value against the political economy. The expansion and production are not quantitative but qualitative, and the multitude is "an irreducible multiplicity"; however, "the singular social differences that constitute the multitude must always be expressed and can never be flattened into sameness, unity, identity, or indifference," constituting not multiple fragments but "singularities that act in common."[22] What is noteworthy here is that the multitude is the counter-concept of the *Urstaat*, the primordial violence of the state form, which is "the eternal model of everything the State wants to be and desires."[23] It is the state that expresses and constitutes the objective movements of production. People are the force of production captured in the state form and, in this sense, another aspect of the multitude. The multitude is nothing less than those who have never been represented by the nation-state, despite living inside the void of the *Urstaat*, which repetitively creates the transcendental outside of a specific state form from within. Unlike MacCannell's structuralist presupposition, modern man's generic condition is, in this sense, not tourist but refugee.

For now, Azuma's question of the multitude remains. The multitude as the dissolution of people could be regarded as ontological resistance to the *Urstaat*, although not automatically militant. Its ontological state is not the only condition of "militant-becoming." Azuma's concept of the tourist tries to solve this problem through its endorsement of small-world and scale-free mathematical models. Small-world networks are typified by local clustering and proximate ties that reduce the distance between clusters, while scale-free networks have an asymmetrical degree of distribution. Therefore, small-world networks serve as equally contingent connections, while scale-free networks function as unequally skewed distribution. According to Azuma, nation-states could be called the small-world network and Empire could be regarded as the scale-free network.[24] The doctrine of the nation-state includes the equality of all national members within their small-worlds, whereas the principle of Empire imposes unequal dissemination of scale-free networks upon the small-worlds. Based on this presupposition, he argues that the tourist is a "political" existence to recuperate the contingency of "misdelivery" between the small-world network and the scale-free network.

Nevertheless, it seems to me that Empire is not simply the mathematical model but the actualization of global capitalism. Even though Empire does the work of the scale-free network, the fundamental inequality of the global order can ultimately be ascribed to capitalism. Empire as a scale-free network would enhance the hierarchical disparity, but politico-economic disparity among nation-states is not the consequence of mathematical law. Darwin's theory of evolution can be adapted to explain how the fittest survive in nature. Yet its application in justification of social meritocracy falls into the trap of ruling class ideology. "Social Darwinism" shows the typical fallacy of such a pseudoscientific exercise. Above all, it is not self-evident that the tourist is a political subject. The common mode for the tourist is as a consumer in high capitalism. It must purchase travel commodities, or become a consumer, in other words, if it wants to encounter the enigmatic other. Travel has the allure of the most popular commodities, and the development of mass transportation has enhanced the travel industry's competition. During recent decades, airfare became the most flexible commodity due to budget tourism. As a member of the nation-state and at the same time a cosmopolitan consumer in Empire, the tourist must fulfill the requirements of global capitalism, i.e., money and the right of travel.

When tourists lose the rights of travel and money, they are forced to be something else: refugees. This is the moment in which the repressed real of global capitalism returns. In this sense, the tourist is another mode of the refugee and vice versa. In fact, the ambiguous status of the tourist is not political in itself; "misdelivery" is the ontological state applicable not only to the tourist but to communication in general. As consumers, tourists want to extend their domains to wherever they visit. The tourist's illusion would break down as it encounters the reality of capitalism and is dissociated from its habitual perception of others. What is necessary for this to occur is *méconnaissance,* the misrecognition of the ego, i.e., the very function of a mirror image. The tourist's ego always seeks its mirror image in others, but this expectation is occasionally complicated by real experience. If the tourist encounters this strangeness by chance, it is no longer who it was. This overdetermined misunderstanding, i.e., one where each cause is necessary to bring forth the effect of *méconnaissance,* is the tourist's existential condition and leads them to the subjectivation of the multitude. In this sense, the militant is not the opposite of the tourist but more likely its qualitatively transformed subject, the monstrous metamorphosis of the consumer. Therefore, what is crucial in the tourist's political reversion is not the mechanism of "misdelivery" as such but its militant subjectivation.

Marx points out that production creates the consumer; "Production not only supplies a material for the need, but it also supplies a need for the material."[25] The tourist as a consumer is also trapped in the category of the labor force, i.e., the commodification of labor power. If a person wants to move from one nation-state to another, they must choose whether they do so as labor commodity or as consumer. Mobility is a key feature of capitalism. The working class is the moveable population and portable labor force, yet it is legally obliged to stay within a specific territory. It is not the labor force but money and commodities that are permitted to travel. Although a commodity can be exchanged for money, the two are not the same. As Marx argues, "The function of money ... is to remain in circulation as its vehicle, to resume its circular course always anew like a *perpetuum mobile*."[26] Monetary circulation enables the mobility of capitalist production, whereas a commodity completes its final function when it is consumed. In other words, consumption means a commodity's retreat from circulation. When a commodity is consumed, its function ends, its form finally annihilates, and money then moves from one territory to another to find different commodities. For this reason, as long as the labor force is a commodity removed from circulation, it has no mobility. Global mobility is fueled by monetary flow; financial flux in the global scope. Nevertheless, the dialectic between monetary circulation and commodity consumption remains bound to the political economy of the *Urstaat*. I contend that this double-bind relationship is the political deadlock of Empire and the nation-state.

3.
The Viral Interpellation

A VIRUS INFECTS NOT ONLY OUR BODIES but also our thought. The impact of the Black Death was crucial to the European transition from feudalism to capitalism and fixed its effect in the popular imagination. Many narratives described the bubonic plague apocalyptically and showed its disastrous consequence. The *magna pestilencia* changed the economic structure and, at the same time, people's perspectives on the world. The pandemic paved the way toward popular uprisings linked to socioeconomic reconstruction. The demographic decline forced institutional change and the redistribution of labor power. The contagion was not the sole cause of the structural transition but a significant factor that accelerated the old regime's collapse.

A virus cannot move by itself, including COVID-19, and it needs a host, i.e., animals. In Latin, *animal* refers to a living being, a being with breath. The symbolic system of human signification already inscribed the secret of the viral epidemic within its cultural origin. An animal transmits a virus to another animal. When, unlike today, animals did not interact with each other regularly, variations of viruses were few. Each virus stayed within each territory; it had an individual host animal belonging to a specific species. Each animal could abide in its terrain, and each virus lingered in each animal horde.

What changed the principle of "territorialization" was human mobility. The Silk Road brought the Black Death from Asia to Europe. However, the European expansion and competition mobilized the Spanish flu pandemic (the virus did not originate in Spain). Not surprisingly, global capitalism is the human vehicle thought to generate the worldwide spread of COVID-19, which we are witnessing in the twenty-first century. No doubt, one of the earliest reports says that the outbreak of the epidemic took place in China; however, the crucial cause of the pandemic was not known when the outbreak of infection occurred in China. Wuhan, one of the most globalized cities in China, was where human-to-human viral transmission occurred.

Many journalists and critics pointed to the Chinese custom of eating wild animals, such as bats, as the mainspring of the plague. This tradition remains in China and other Southeast Asian countries such as Indonesia. Yet daily exposure to zoonotic infection had not whipped up pandemics as quickly as the outbreak of COVID-19 occurred in those countries. The human mobility of a globalized city such as Wuhan precipitated the pervasive dissemination of the virus beyond borders. According to a recent medical report, in the case of COVID-19, novel coronavirus-infected pneumonia (NCIP), there was "the apparent presence of many mild infections" and "limited resources for isolation of cases and quarantine of their close contacts," thus challenging the potential to take control of the situation.[1] COVID-19's moderate symptoms distinguish it from other viral cases like SARS.

It is clear that the Chinese government ignored the early alarms sounded by the region and did not listen to the experts in the city. The authorities repressed the public circulation of information regarding what had happened in Wuhan. Much criticism focused on the authoritarian attitude, in other words, the inefficiency of the non-democratic system of the Chinese government. For instance, in the *New York Times*, Steven Lee Myers claimed that China's lack of transparency was the main reason for the failure of quarantine. After the contagion of SARS, he states, the Chinese government proudly announced that China had set in place a world-class infectious disease reporting system. However, the system did not work. To support his presupposition, Myers quoted one study, which argues that if the Chinese government had implemented more aggressive action a week earlier in the epidemic stage, the ratio of infections could have dropped much lower.[2] However, this quotation arouses a paradox in his argument.

What should be questioned here is the meaning of the "aggressive action" posited by Myers. Does it mean that the Chinese government should have responded to the alert system and permitted public circulation of the information by journalists and on social media? Does it mean that the local authority should have recommended that people in Wuhan stay home to prevent the epidemic and asked those with infections to report their symptoms to a medical center? Ironically, "aggressive action" does not imply such a democratic quarantine. In this sense, Myers's argument is an attempt to square the circle. If the Chinese government had immediately responded to the warning system, what would have happened?

Many political reasons might have prevented them from acting aggressively. We can consider some now, but it does not seem that insufficient freedom is one of these reasons, despite Myers's assumptions. Freedom is not necessarily compatible with quarantine. It is undeniable that China's accomplishment in reversing its earlier failings and containing the situation seems to lie in its extreme shutdown of human mobility. On the contrary, Europe and the US, which did not follow the Chinese model, chased the epidemic's uncontrollable outburst. The case in China and others in Taiwan, Singapore, and even South Korea prove that freedom is an obstacle to controlling human-to-human transmission.

The problem is not China's withholding of infection information from the public and instead stems from *an absent cause* that led the Chinese government to halt "aggressive action" in the early stage of the plague. What would it be? I would say that it is an economic cause. As a gigantic factory for the global market,

Chinese politics is closely related to its economic growth, appeasing the demand of its middle class, which seems to support the current political regime. Wuhan is a highly globalized city and the hub of transport and industry for central China. The town is the thoroughfare of global capitalism located in the country's heartland, and its shutdown would significantly impact China's economy.[3] Therefore, China's miscarriage early in the outbreak of COVID-19 resides in neither the absence of democracy nor systemic inefficiency but within global capitalism itself, a destructive system sustained through the sacrifice of local community for the hypermobility of capital. This fact has nothing to do with whether or not China is democratic.

Global Capitalism and Pandemic

The COVID-19 pandemic is the consequence of globally mobilizing capitalism. It jeopardizes the globalists' belief in market universalism imposed by unified trade rules, i.e., the dream of a neoliberal paradise worldwide. The recent debate between Slavoj Žižek and Byung-Chul Han revolves around this issue. Žižek writes that "the coronavirus epidemic is a kind of '*Five Point Palm Exploding Heart Technique*' attack on the global capitalist system – a signal that we cannot go on the way we were up until now; a radical change is needed."[4] Referring to *Kill Bill*, Žižek borrows a term from martial art fantasy, the deadly blow of the *Five Point Palm Exploding Heart Technique*, to describe the COVID-19 effect, which facilitates the fundamental crisis of global capitalism. To him, the pandemic that stems from this biological virus brings forth an epidemic explosion of ideological viruses latent within the paradise of global capitalism, such as fake news, conspiracy theories and racism.

Žižek concludes that today's pandemic invites us to reconsider global capitalism's radical change and to reinvent communism.

To him, the rebooting of communism at this moment is the only solution able to meet such urgent demand. He fleshes out this argument further and tries to convince us by clarifying his initial concept of communism.[5] Žižek's point is that the communist task of solving the economic crisis caused by the global pandemic is already being undertaken by those who have never been communists: Boris Johnson, the prime minister of England, for instance. For Žižek, communism is not a hazy dream but a "name" for what is already going on, i.e., a new master-signifier to indicate that which has no place in current politics but which has always coexisted as the void of global capitalism. Against Žižek's appeal for the reinvention of communism, Byung-Chul Han declares that Žižek is wrong because global capitalism will be restored vigorously soon after this crisis and the virus cannot cause us to "think" or "re-think" politics.[6] Drawing on Naomi Klein's shock doctrine theory, Han argues that the state of emergency always serves as an excuse for a more enhanced system of government. Han warns that even Europe will regard the Chinese model as a successful system against the pandemic and go on to import the digital police state for its security after this turbulence.

Han's position here seems to resonate with the perspectives of Giorgio Agamben and Roberto Esposito: both identify emergency as the pretext for the exceptional enaction of authoritarian regimes. Further unified in belief, both Han and Esposito share visions of China as the future of Europe. Echoing Han's concern, Esposito claims that the drift toward a state of exception "tends to bring the political procedures of democratic regimes into conformity with those of authoritarian states, such as China."[7] What is missing in their ideas is that China is not the future of Europe but instead the real face of global capitalism in which Europe has already participated. The reality of this pandemic proves that European exceptionalism no longer exists.

High Technology and Primitive Exploitation

Susan Watkins's analysis of the EU delineates how today's Europe has come to exist. A set of structural torsions encircled three dimensions in the European polity since the 1970s: "civic-democratic relations, between the rulers and the ruled; inter-state relations, between the member countries; and geopolitical relations, characterizing the bloc's external role."[8] Pressure from the outside, e.g., "the collapse of the Bretton Woods system in the early seventies, the fall of the Soviet bloc in the nineties, and the world financial crisis that exploded in 2008," enforced these structural distortions upon Europe.

The transformations of Europe each, in turn, corresponded to the neoliberal reformation of labor, globalization with the rise of China, and debt-logged stagnation after 2008. Europe is already part of global capitalism, not exceptional to the high-speed economic system. The decline of European values seems obvious: the 2015 Charlie Hebdo attacks marked the disturbing truth that Europe's privileged sense of freedom of expression is no longer self-evident. As Étienne Balibar states, the shooting teaches Europe that it must cost one's own life. In short, Europe today can no longer enjoy watching the conflicts between two parties whilst sitting on the fence.

Han's problem lies in something more than this ignorant confusion. His diagnosis of why China and other Asian countries, such as South Korea, Taiwan, and Singapore, have succeeded in decreasing the speed of the viral spread has no grounds to support his arguments. He marks out the advantages of Asia as an "authoritarian mentality." As maintained by his analysis, Asian people are more obedient to state power, and their daily life is disciplined strictly by digital surveillance. He underlines the Confucian tradition embedded in these Asian regimes to explain such Asian compliance with the panopticon authority. However, his logic quickly betrays this weak point when considering the South Korean case of viral epidemics.

His observation lacks acknowledgement of South Korea's success in managing the infections via *the invisible hand* behind the scenes of the government's propaganda. As a person living in the country, I have found that not all people obey the government's directions; some even trick digital surveillance. If the infection rate is not high, it is not because of a Confucian tradition and digital Big Brother but due to low-waged public health workers and civil servants mobilized by the government. Controlling COVID-19 in South Korea relies on cutting-edge technology and the very primitive exploitation of labor power. Workers check on each person who is supposed to be in self-quarantine. They even have a responsibility to search for those who violate the rule of self-quarantine. Digital technology is a valuable supplement for manual labor, not the central platform to administrate the people.

Ironically, the South Korean "authoritarian mentality," which Han points out as the backdrop for South Korean achievement, was constructed through Japanese colonialism and the Cold War. During those periods, the anticommunist dictatorship brought the capitalist mode of production into the country. The legacy of anticommunism today in the form of submission to authoritarian state power is well equipped for neoliberalism. In this sense, the primary aspect of the South Korean economic system can be called authoritarian capitalism, in that the central government is in the driver's seat to rein in the market. However, this authoritarian appearance does not mean that South Korea is a totalitarian country. The right question here might be why such authoritarian collectivism has been in harmony with global capitalism. Of course, this question applies not only to South Korea but to all Asian countries, including Japan.

Han's critique of Žižek's communism is also obsessed with the former's preconception of totalitarianism. What Žižek tries to say is that the notion seems not to justify totalitarian regimes but to remind us of social mutualism, not in Proudhon's sense but in Fourier's. Fourier's "mutualism" is the romantic cosmology of communism, not limited to economic theory. In my opinion, communism is the transcendental use of utopianism, and today's urgent demand is to reinvent or repeat, in Gilles Deleuze's sense, its pure mutualism. The paradise of global capitalism, i.e., capitalism without the working class, means that anything goes except communism. However, what if someone attempted to exercise pure mutualism, the idea of free association with all life, against global capitalism? Global pandemics urge us to build international cooperation beyond nation-states and think about a new internationalism in the ruins of today's political failures.

As Han concludes, radical changes to global capitalism are brought forth not by the virus but by the political subjectivity of mutual association, association in which everyone is equal. Each being is not merely human as a reasoning animal but is a bearer to negotiate the condition of reason with the transcendental idea of the present dystopia. It is neither the virus nor reason but the idea that leads us toward reinventing the world after this global pandemic.

4.
Zombie and Demos

THE KOREAN ZOMBIE CRAZE has suddenly begun to attract global attention. *Train to Busan* (2016) was its beginning point, and this trend culminated in the extreme fascination with the Netflix series *Kingdom* (2019). The zombie genre is not popular in Asian countries, even to this day, whereas ghost stories still dominate the mainstream cultural market. Contrary to ghost fantasy, which is instead based on romantic imagination, the logic of the zombie genre is more inclined toward science fiction. There are always scientific reasons for the genesis of zombies, such as radioactive repercussions, viral pandemics, chemical pollution, etc. Scientific knowledge is usually applied to link zombies and their conditions in these fictional narratives.

Another reason for the Asian indifference to the Hollywood genre would be its political rhetoric, which is not yet adaptable to the "Asiatic mode of production." Since George A. Romero's film *Night of the Living Dead* (1968), the zombie has served as a popular allegory for the critique of so-called late capitalism. The genre as such waned for a while but was widely revived in the 1990s, growing in popularity after the rise of video games such as *Resident Evil* and *The House of the Dead*. Zombies, and the colonial otherness of non-Europe, then turned into the monstrous figure of consumerism and its unstoppable greed. In *Dawn of the Dead* (1978), Romero's sequel to *Night of the Living Dead*, a shopping mall is described as the hell of cannibalistic capitalism, in which the living dead walk around without agency. Yet the zombie is not the only horrific figure to remind us of the cruel reality of capitalism.

Karl Marx used the metaphor of the vampire to portray the capitalist exploitation of the working class. He claimed that "capital is dead labour, which, vampire-like, lives only by sucking living labour, and lives the more, the more labour it sucks."[1] Marx's metaphor of the vampire also indicated the imperialist expansion of the European bourgeoisie to the other territories and the reproduction of their mirror image all over the non-European lands. This lifeforce-draining lust for self-cloning is the essence of the vampire-like capitalist, which Bram Stoker described well in his novel *Dracula*. After being captured by the immortal creature, Mina became like Count Dracula in the story. Vampires transfuse their blood into a victim by sucking its blood. The purpose of their survival is the spread of their species. In a similar manner, the self-replication of the bourgeoisie, like the vampire, is the secret of capitalism.

Both the vampire and the zombie are common rhetorical adaptations for criticizing capitalism, but there is an undeniable difference between them. What separates the vampire from the zombie is its aristocratic nature. The vampire is bourgeois—the colonizer—while the zombie is the working class—the colonized. That is to say, the vampire is Robinson Crusoe, while the zombie, on the other hand, is Friday. The story of the vampire stems from the romantic figure of eighteen-century individualism, but the legend of the zombie was imported from colonized Haiti. The zombie has no self and lacks the dignity of the high-class vampire. The zombie does not exist alone but is instead described as part of a mob. Unlike the zombie, the vampire is ascribed to its mythological origin.

I would say that the vampire is an economic metaphor, whereas the zombie is a political allegory, the incarnation of baroque melancholia in Walter Benjamin's sense. The allegory of the zombie can be grasped as a *Trauerspiel*, the mourning play of "baroque capitalism." What is baroque capitalism? There has been some discussion today, which resonates with accelerationism, regarding the high-capitalist style as the form of social progress that could leverage the capitalist mode of production and transcend the limits of economic accumulation. According to a critic like Toby Shorin, "The accelerationist movement and baroque capitalism mirror one another."[2] The style of baroque capitalism goes beyond the modernist restrictions of form and praises the growth of capital. Its stylish realization comes to a climax in flamboyant architectural decorations like those of the Trump building. In this sense, baroque capitalism is "the aesthetic which allows the unchallenged domination of capital to best express itself, presenting itself at its highest level of accumulation, as pure generative and expressive force, freed from all constraints and constrictions."[3]

Of course, this observation about baroque capitalism would prove to be the partial truth of today's "pure capitalism," but its accelerationist point of view is problematic; the accelerationist approach to economic accumulation is nothing other than the aestheticization of capitalism as such. It would make sense if such a notion were used to describe the crucial feature of baroque capitalism as extreme aestheticism. However, the aesthetic exercise is always paired with the practice of political economy. The aesthetic aspect of baroque capitalism is the ideological apparatus that controls labor power. Capitalist accumulation is impossible if there is no living labor. This living labor is an actual worker alive in time. Therefore, the blood for the voracious appetite of the capitalist vampire is "surplus labour-time," and only with this can the metaphor of the vampire be an adequate trope that explains the capitalist exploitation of labor. Contrary to the accelerationist presupposition, capitalism cannot express itself fully without a worker's blood, i.e., surplus labor time.

Marx says, "Wherever a part of society possesses the monopoly of the means of production, the worker, free or unfree, must add to the labour-time necessary for his own maintenance an extra quantity of labour-time in order to produce the means of subsistence for the owner of the means of production."[4] There is no capitalist who is willing to make up for this surplus labor time. Marx's analysis of the working day reveals how even baroque capitalism controls the workplace and then profits from the individual workers. For this reason, the acceleration of its productive force cannot surpass the limit of capitalist accumulation. In this sense, the edge of capitalism lies in the proletariat, not the bourgeoisie. All variations of the early capitalist mode of production, such as cognitive capitalism and surveillance capitalism, emerged from strategic modification of surplus labor-time exploitation. Upon leaving the workplace, the worker becomes a consumer, and these two modes of existence constitute the ambiguity of baroque capitalism.

Here, I would like to employ the term *baroque* to recall the original meaning of Catholic *dispositif*, the implosion of its logic from within. Benjamin's concept of *Trauerspiel* could be understood as an inverted form of religious propaganda. In the melancholic drama, there is no God, only the undead, i.e., the specter of the father and the haunted son, as in the case of *Hamlet*. Baroque capitalism is the aestheticization of its vampire-like accumulation, which transforms the worker into a zombie. The zombie is the embodiment of melancholia and the theatricalization of the capitalist ontology.

The theme of the zombie is the return of the medieval macabre, the eschatological symbol of death, which remains a melancholic character because it cannot die. What is absent in the modern macabre is, ironically, death itself. This deathlessness of the undead is what Slavoj Žižek calls the death drive. However, the existence of the zombie as an allegory has political implications beyond its symbolic logic. Unlike the metaphor of the vampire, which romanticizes bourgeois individualism, the allegory of the zombie designates the hatred of the fallen working class and the monstrosity of pure capitalism.

Gilles Deleuze and Félix Guattari correctly point out that "the myth of the zombie, of the living dead, is a work myth and not a war myth."[5] The war machine embedded in the capitalist state—i.e., the police and the military—endlessly produces zombies, and the zombie-like mode of existence is "a necessary condition of the State apparatus and the organization of work."[6] More interestingly, the recent Korean zombie genre, which includes *Train to Busan* and *Kingdom,* describes the state as the venue where constant civil war mutilates people and renders them crippled. Far from the Hobbesian presupposition, this allegorical intervention into *realpolitik* reveals that the state is not guaranteed by a secured social contract but is instead sustained through the dramatization of the zombie myth, i.e., the politics of fear. In my view, the representation of Korean zombies emphasize the site of high capitalism, where the baroque allegory plays out.

Zombies are the dismembered demos, the juridically policed capacity, which has no part in the state. The traditional goal of capitalism was to reproduce the bourgeois vampire, but today's capitalism does not breed the bloodsucker. The aestheticization of current capitalist accumulation suppresses mass protests by portraying civil unrest through frightening zombie imagery. However, the unstoppable hunger of the defeated working class cannot be sated by this propaganda due to its primal scene, the repression of the death drive, unless the baroque allegory is realized as an event.

5.
BTS and the Nation-State

ON OCTOBER 26, 2018, *Tokyo Sports*, a well-known right-wing newspaper in Japan, reported that Jimin, a member of the mega-popular Korean boy band BTS, wore a T-shirt bearing an image of the atomic bombing of Nagasaki and Hiroshima during World War II. The newspaper insisted that Japan cancel BTS's visit and their scheduled performance at the Tokyo Dome. Jimin apologized for his ignorance regarding the symbolic meaning of the shirt and promised his Japanese fans that he would mull over the violence of the warfare more carefully. He did not admit to any political aim with the shirt, claiming he simply wore it to show respect for a fan who had sent it to him. However, the words on the shirt were "Patriotism, Our History, Liberation, Korea," a slogan to justify nationalist sentiment in the country. Whatever his real motivation was, the incident was quickly attributed to Jimin's naivety, and his expression of regret ended the controversy. However, I argue that the episode was not accidental but was instead the consequence of a paradox between nationalism and cosmopolitanism in global capitalism.

As a global commodity, BTS should be cosmopolitan; nevertheless, they cannot transcend their nationality as members of a nation-state. Jimin's act of commemorating Korea's National Liberation Day by wearing the shirt not only enraged Japanese nationalists but also sparked heated debate among BTS fans in Japan about the shirt's message.

The phrases printed on the shirt appeared to support the deployment by the United States of atomic bombs against Japan, which pacifist Dorothy Day described as a "colossal slaughter of the innocents." At the same time, worldwide news organizations such as the *BBC*, *CNN*, and *The Guardian* were drawn to the message on the shirt. They speculated that Jimin wore the shirt in question to express a political opinion influenced by rising tensions between South Korea and Japan. However, Big Hit Entertainment, the organization that manages BTS, stressed that Jimin's printed garments were not for political purposes.

The company insisted that the artist was not responsible for the message since he had no intention of provoking a dispute. In short, the company seemed to confirm that Jimin was clueless about the deeper meaning of the commemorative gift and that his deviation resulted from a naive attitude toward *realpolitik*. Their clarification formed a standard response to such negative criticism, but in my opinion, their answer marks the beginning of another problem, not the conclusion of the conflict. If the proclamation about Jimin's deed is correct, he is nothing other than an immature person who cannot understand the humanitarian issues concerning the atomic bombing. This result makes BTS's ethical statement about their love for humanity suspect. As is generally known, they were invited to speak before the United Nations General Assembly and were awarded the Order of Cultural Merit by the Korean government. As a result, Jimin's lack of awareness of humanistic concerns clashes with BTS's normative image thus far.

Meanwhile, things would worsen if the announcement was wrong and Jimin knew its political implication well. This would mean that both he and his management lied to people in order to quickly extricate themselves from difficulties. Jimin would have had the friendly intention of wearing the shirt in order to acknowledge the fan who sent it to him . His deed was not politically wrong and morally right. However, the effect of the action brought forth an unpredictable result. Why did this disturbance take place? Of course, it is not Jimin's fault. Some journalists in

South Korea have argued that BTS must establish more practical strategies for the global market by diluting its "Korean-ness." This kind of business advice bluntly reveals the symbolic implication of BTS and other K-pop industries. Even these journalists are convinced that BTS is a commodity for the global market and that it needs to erase its nationality tactically. Quite to the contrary, the episode involving Jimin's shirt was not caused by a musician's lack of strategic approach to the global market but by the iron cage of the dialectical relationship between nationalism and cosmopolitanism. The vicious circle of identity is where the national question arises. In this sense, the problem of BTS has nothing to do with individual virtue but instead results from structural overdetermination revolving around a nation-state.

Cosmopolitanism is an Enlightenment idea, which aims at the production of modern civil society. Kant argues that a host's hospitality can guarantee cosmopolitanism for his guest.[1] The point is that personal kindness rests not on philanthropic generosity but on the "right to visit, to which all human beings have a claim, to present oneself to society by virtue of the right of common possession of the surface of the earth."[2] However, Kant did not know that nation-states would come to control this common right. After World War I, the temporary imposition of passport controls became permanent, and the laissez-faire era of international migration ended.[3] Nationality relies on the technical partition of the common right. Kant thought that the right to travel across territories is self-evident; yet the request needs another right, i.e., the political right to insist upon the right to visit or reside in any nation-state. The dispute involving Jimin's shirt revealed the clash between nationalism and cosmopolitanism, but still, the episode does not mean the two values are incompatible. As Hannah Arendt points out, "once they had left their homeland they remained homeless, once they had left their state they became stateless; once they had been deprived of their human rights, they were rightless, the scum of the earth."[4] In other words, a nation-state provides the foundation for such a common right, the condition of humanity, which can allow anyone the legitimacy to enter or leave through the border.

Two historical arguments regarding nation-states might be considered here; first, the conservative viewpoint that "the nation-state is the 'realized' form of the nation, that nations without corresponding states remain frozen in a form of infancy," and second, the Marxist position that "the tendency toward the articulation between the nation and the state is an effect of the development of capitalism."[5] Jimin's position would be close to the former, i.e., the traditionalist understanding of the nation-state. However, this identification of the nation with the establishment of the state is unsuited to cosmopolitanism. If, following this logic, there is no cosmopolitanism without the nation-state, the nation-state is the materialization of the nation—the juridico-political substance of an imagined community. For this reason, Jimin would believe that he did the right thing when celebrating National Liberation Day. Still, the disturbing truth is revealed when the national romance regards Japan as the nation's enemy. From the perspective of this Manichean dichotomy, any form of violence against the enemy is best—the more ruthless, the better for us. Nationalism cannot justify its logic from within but instead gains its meaning by defining the enemy from without.

On the contrary, however, there is a fundamental discrepancy between the nation-state and the nation of the imaginary, yet nationalism as fantasy seals the split seamlessly. The ideological unity of the nation and the state is inevitably disrupted by capitalism. In this view, nationalism is an intellectual interpellation to develop the subjects of the nation-state and advance the imagined basis for legal nationality.

Nationality is the precondition for human rights. A man's right is not automatically given by natural law but is instead obtained through the citizenship tied to nationality. Unlike Kant's proposition, cosmopolitan citizenship is founded on the paradox of the human ontology in the modern age; we, human beings, have no self-evident right to reside in any place without nationality, even if we travel across international borders. There is no such thing as the absolute right of self-determination except in the historical phenomenon of the nation-state. Nationality is the real border in the age of the nation-state. Those who have no right to reside within the boundaries will be regarded as "the scum of the earth." Those with this stateless status are called refugees. In my opinion, the existence of refugees proves how the nation-state serves as a form of capitalist accumulation. Refugees, who do not have any national identification, are as reckless as the waste. They have no legal right that allows them to work in a nation-state. Refugees are useless because they are not exchangeable within the national mode of production. If any refugee desires to be exchanged, they must commodify themselves. The commodification of their labor power is their only means of existence in capitalism. Citizenship provides the legal right to sell living labor in a nation-state. However, the case of BTS clarifies that juridico-politics must approve any commodity produced by a nation-state. Of course, the commodity goes global, but its trade or sale must be allowed by juridical approval. As Karl Marx points out, "Commodities cannot themselves go to market and perform exchanges in their own right."[6] This juridical relation is nothing other than a contract between different individual wills, which depends on the economic relation. Based on this contract, each person exists as a representative and an owner of any commodity.

The early twentieth century saw "extraordinary upheavals concerning the form of the nation," and this begat "the assertion of new linguistic sovereignties and newly discovered national borders."[7] The establishment of a common language within a specific territory is necessary for national formation. In this sense, the invention of the nation is related to the imaginary fabrication of a nationalist story. Étienne Balibar and Immanuel Wallerstein point out that "the history of nations, beginning with our own, is always already presented to us in the form of a narrative which attributes to these entities the continuity of a subject."[8] The relationship between the nation and each subject is presented in a narrative form. However, this nation-form as a narrative is immanent in the nation's construction. As Balibar clarifies, the nation-form is the assemblage of apparatuses and practices that initiate an individual as "*homo nationalis* from cradle to grave."[9]

The nation-form is the interpellation of the subject or the subjectification of the individual. The imaginary nation or community of the past never exists but is perpetually invented through the myth of origins and national continuity. Therefore, "the formation of the nation ... appears as the fulfillment of a 'project' stretching over centuries, in which there are different stages and moments of coming to self-awareness."[10] The establishment of a nation-state is the consequence of contingent events, which have nothing to do with the cause or destiny of the nation. Nations have no historical lineage or experience, but their myth of the national golden age is created by nationalism. Nationalism has been used to mobilize "free" individuals in the modern state. The national orientation is the by-product of capitalism, even though its sentiment seems firmly rooted in the mythical origins.

Interestingly, Marx discussed how the invention of the individual serves as the precondition for production in his famous introduction to the critique of political economy. After stating that "the subject of our discussion is first of all *material* production by individuals as determined by society," Marx goes on to criticize the starting point for Smith and Ricardo: "the individual and isolated hunter or fisher," i.e., "the insipid illusions of the eighteenth century."[11] To quote Marx,

They are Robinsonades which do not by any means represent, as students of the history of civilization imagine, a reaction against over-refinement and a return to a misunderstood natural life. They are no more based on such a naturalism than is Rosseau's "contrat social," which makes naturally independent individuals come in contract and have mutual intercourse by contract. They are the fiction and only the aesthetic fiction of the small and great Robinsonades.[12]

Indeed, the narrative of Robinson Crusoe anticipates the stereotype of the bourgeois personality in the capitalist mode of production, giving rise to the model of the individual. Marx points up the long-lasting illusion that the individual is a product of nature, not of history. Belief in the free individual is the foundation of classical economics. However, the individual isolated from society is simply a myth. Marx emphasized that whenever we speak of production, "we always have in mind production at a certain stage of social development, or production by social individuals."[13] For this reason, production corresponds to a specific historical period. Marx's point lies in understanding production as the historical process of economic development, i.e., the analysis of modern capitalist production, which, for Marx, "constitutes the subject proper of this work."[14] The investigation aims to illuminate the common purposes in all modes of production.

What are the features shared by all modes of production? These general elements, present throughout the different historical stages of production, are "the subject, mankind, and the object, nature."[15] What is necessary for production is labor (the subject) and the instrument (the object). As a matter of fact, the instrument of production is the accumulation of labor in the past. As for the mode of capitalism, capital as an instrument of production is "a universal, eternal natural phenomenon."[16] In this way, Marx recognized the role of political economy in mobilizing individuals into *homo nationalis*. Marx criticizes social contract theory and argues that all contracts are artificial. What is important is what or who decides the terms and conditions of the contract. Marx's critique of political economy clarifies that "all economists" emphasize "property" and "the protection of the latter by the administration of justice, police, etc."[17] Therefore, political economy has nothing to do with a specific stage of productive arrangement. There is a fundamental discrepancy between political economy and the forms of production. The connection between the general ends of production and the discrete forms of production will be developed constantly afterward, not designed beforehand by the economic theory. In other words, economics is nothing but the retroactive theory of actual production. This argument implies that the nation-state is a political suture between nation and state.

This observation leads us to understand the fandom around BTS. Fan activity intervenes in the legal relationship between BTS and Big Hit. As a cultural commodity, consumers cannot own BTS as such, and the contract belongs to the relation between BTS and Big Hit Entertainment. The only thing fans can do within the monetary exchange system is to enjoy the consumption of the volatile moments of BTS's performances. Today's development of telecommunication technology, i.e., social media and streaming services, makes it possible to retain temporal experiences via "digital tertiary retention" in Stiegler's sense.[18] Audiences can watch what they want at any time by replaying recorded performances. However, they do not want to give up the authentic relationship with their idols. Technology provides a medium that enables them to sustain their feelings continuously. In this vein, BTS fandom, i.e., the BTS ARMY, runs counter to the contract. Its relation to BTS is not a profit-based bond but rather an affinity beyond economic interest.

To a certain extent, the emotional consumption of idols is useless, and I believe this uselessness is the political implication of BTS fandom. It would be true that BTS fans voluntarily participate in social issues and political agendas under the name of BTS's supporters. They use BTS as a channel through which they practice global solidarity and recognize their transnational citizenship. The creation of the transnational zone is the purpose of their participation in BTS's fandom. I would say that the BTS ARMY's enjoyment is not ascribed to the excess of desire but rather the delegation of desire to the object. Ironically, this regressive wish hinders realization of the fantasy and passes their desire on to their idols. It is as if they act, but they do not.

This transference means not vicarious satisfaction but double delegation, which creates the representative agent of pleasure and the rituals with which to hand down belief in the illusion to an undefined other. BTS fans want nothing but to consume the cultural commodity without any belief. In this sense, their behavior might be regarded as an ideological response to capitalist nihilism. This nihilism would be related to capitalism's "anarchistic turn" in Catherine Malabou's sense, which marks "decentralized currencies, the end of the state's monopoly, the obsolescence of the mediating role played by banks, and the decentralization of exchanges and transaction."[19] This horizontal anarchism of global capitalism arouses the hierarchical movements of populism within nation-states, which justify national identity or authenticity. The attempt to bring forth the depth of the nation resists the decentralization of political economy.

Contrary to this inclination, the orientation of BTS fandom seems to have a different destination. The fandom reveals the depthlessness of global capitalism against nationalism. The fans want to act not as subjects but as delegates of their desire. What they desire is not the fulfillment of their wanting but the constant state of desiring. They are not interested in the object of the desire, instead craving deference of the pleasure of the desire, for they must stop desiring if they could easily own the object. BTS is not only a cultural commodity but also an intangible object beyond the pleasure principle. The emotional response of fans to the graven image resembles the response to a magic show rather than a response to participation in a religious rite. The fans enjoy it but do not believe in the presence of a miracle. They consider themselves ordinary people, but as Jacques Rancière points out, "The common people *are* the army."[20] In this sense, I believe the BTS ARMY is a symbolic answer to the disenchantment that results from the process of commodification. The ARMY does not love BTS as a commercial product but rather wishes to sustain the magical illusion it has staged through the boys' fiction.

6.
The Desire
of *Squid Game*

ON OCTOBER 12, 2021, Arirang Meari, a North Korean propaganda website, said that Netflix's global smash-hit *Squid Game* discloses the "beastly capitalism" of South Korea, where corruption and rogues are everywhere. The nine-episode thriller made in South Korea, now a worldwide sensation for Netflix, has encouraged not only the North Korean demagogue but also many critics across the world to write about its mirror image of the cruel reality of capitalism. Cobbling together details from *Battle Royale, As the Gods Will,* and *The Hunger Games,* the Korean drama series succeeded in elevating its theatrical visual effect beyond mere reference. Despite its extremely gory images, the flatness of its characters, and the absence of a plausible narrative, the Korean-made cultural product ranked as the most popular series on Netflix. Through its success, *Squid Game* has helped boost Netflix subscriptions and raise stakes for the company in the broadband battle.

Many observers, at least in North Korean media, share a common presupposition that the dramatic plot corresponds to the social reality of South Korea—debt-ridden people committed to a deadly competition; dying without any help. These perspectives, including that of North Korean agitprop, do not hesitate to identify the allegory of the zero-sum game with the cruel violence of capitalism. Indeed, most viewers readily accept that the show's dramatic setting aims to criticize capitalism; yet my suspicion of it arises here. There is an intriguing clue in the object *Squid Game* tends to talk about—the Korean collection of Jacques Lacan's writings, titled *The Theory of Desire*, that lays on a desk. The

Korean translation of Lacan's eleventh seminar is also shown in the same scene. Another book laid beside *The Theory of Desire* is an artbook of René Magritte's paintings. These books allude to an ethical conclusion for the sensational spectacle. No doubt, such a clunky dramatic device reveals the director's manipulation and their hidden motivation.

So, the Korean thriller overtly reveals its intention to deal with the problem of desire and its relation to the survival game. On the surface, its purpose seems to criticize capitalism, which instigates the brutal reality of the debt economy. To be sure, *Squid Game* does not hide its political inclination toward denouncing the neoliberal making of the indebted poor. However, it is hard to admit that the drama rigorously tackles the structural inequality of capitalism. Instead, it emphasizes how individual violations of the rules destroy justice within the game. The story's main argument is not for the abolition of disparities but for the establishment of just laws.

This perspective is closer to that of Jeremy Bentham than to Marx, in that its narrative describes the process of the game not as a class struggle but as a panopticon managing discipline and allocating punishment. Bentham called this prison the Inspection House or *Elaboratory*, the purpose of its architecture being the discipline of troublemaking individuals. Its circular surveillance system must work well for the rehabilitation of outlaws. The necessary element for the house of correction is the principle of inspection. According to Bentham, "the more constantly the persons to be inspected are under the eyes of the persons who should inspect them, the more perfectly will the purpose of the establishment have been attained."[1] The crucial element in the penitentiary mechanism is the inspector's impartial role, where the likelihood of being observed remains constant for all inmates.

Squid Game demonstrates how the tenet of the panopticon controls people under the regime of voluntary obedience.

Contrary to the North Korean analysis, its dramatic configuration of Korean society is not about the reflection of cruel capitalism but is instead about the ideological reproduction of reality. Furthermore, the Netflix series, despite its apparent criticism of surveillance capitalism, ultimately targets only illegal business practices. It is these violations, not capitalism itself, that are presented as the real threat to the economic system. Gi-hun's decision in the final scene could be understood as an alibi for the sequel to the series and at the same time a dramatic plot twist that reveals the central theme of its narrative. In short, *Squid Game* is nothing more than a didactic play to punish the poor people who deliberately breach the rules of a fair game. It seems that its symbolic representation of Korean high capitalism analyzes the problem of desire with Lacanian creed, and yet, its description of desire is much closer to that of utilitarian liberalism.

The principle of any game relies on the equal opportunity for luck, as in the case of a lottery. However, Gi-hun finally finds out that the unfair inspectors have cheated him and taken advantage of his goodwill. He also realizes that the founder of the panopticon, contrary to Bentham's expectation, does not believe in the possibility of the Good Samaritan. Gi-hun spews bile at the inequitable rules of the game. What motivates Gi-hun is not so much money as it is gambling, even though it is his poverty that leads him to participate in the Malthusian rat race. The final scene clarifies that he decides to return to the game because of his wrath. Why does he return to the death game when he's on the verge of escape? Why does he give up his freedom and risk his life again? It is as if the heroic moment tied to a free man's courage changes Gi-hun, but the hidden impetus behind the decision is his feeling of guilt. His ambiguous action has nothing to do with morality, instead revealing his desire to continue the game as such—he cannot give up his obsession with death-driven pleasure. Gi-hun's ethical gesture is designed to conceal this real obscenity.

It follows that *Squid Game* does not provide us with a fundamental critique of capitalism. Its primary focus is on the justness of the game, not the rejection of deadly competition. Gi-hun's moral epiphany emphasizes that the just application of the same rule to all participants is necessary for distributing pleasure and implementing justice. The actual message that lurks in this utilitarian backdrop is about the punishment of the poor—the pack of villains who ruin fair competition. The disturbing narrative continuously devises moronic reasons for their elimination from the game. The scandalous description of the wealthy spectators reiterates the pornographic cliché of bourgeois literature: the rich do not want to profit from the game but merely watch it for enjoyment. Certainly, this story does not tell us anything about the capitalist mode of production.

What interests me here is why this Korean drama has widely been perceived as anticapitalist. Why has this Korean-made Netflix original series gained vast popularity across the world? In his recent interview with *El País*, a Spanish media outlet based in Madrid, Byung-Chul Han argues that the global popularity of *Squid Game* indicates total domination and represents "a central aspect of capitalism in an extreme form."[2] Han's understanding of the Netflix series is not far from the North Korean media's vulgar realism. Han and the North Korean propaganda machine both overlook the fact that the South Korean interpretation of capitalism in its drama productions does not simply reflect the social reality. Symbolic representation is part of the reality as such, where the Real of capitalism cannot be fully included within its formal logic. Adapting Slavoj Žižek's terms, *Squid Game* is nothing more than perverted art designed to hide the obscene reality of capitalism from our daily life, i.e., we do not really want what we think we desire. What we want is the sustainable state of desiring as such. Unlike Han's presupposition, *Squid Game* exhibits not the total completion of capitalism but the ideological deception of the culture industry.

There is a homeostasis of capitalist perversion in this mechanism. Capitalism sells a critique of capitalism. Even Netflix produces and distributes *The Social Dilemma*, a documentary that criticizes the big data industry that includes Netflix itself. This paradox does not mean that capitalism totalizes our unconscious. Instead, it implies that we enjoy the "interpassivity" of voluntary obedience to the regime. Endorsing Žižek, Robert Pfaller points out that "interpassive people [seem] to avoid their desire and to transfer it instead to other people, animals, machines and so on" for their pleasure.[3] The concept of interpassivity explains a way of gaining enjoyment by renouncing our freedom to choose. If you think of interpassive arrangements in the case of *Squid Game*, you will see that its dramatic setting provides for its inherent reception. Before we start to watch, we already "know" the problem of capitalism that the Netflix product is supposed to show us. In this actualization of media, i.e., the mechanical operation of online streaming, our participation in the process as a Netflix spectator turns out to be mere excess. In other words, the inner logic of the Netflix series (the utilitarian critique of excessive desire, such as the subduction of unfair enjoyment from the distribution of pleasure) consummates itself without audiences in its realization.

By enjoying *Squid Game*, we can refrain from our surplus appreciation of capitalist obscenity and hand it over to Netflix. This disinterested mode of delaying the fulfillment of our desire is the ideological entailment of new media. The normalization of surplus desire seems to reach even higher level in the interpassive arrangements of an algorithmic mechanism. Now you do not need to think about what you should watch. More than that, you do not need to desire what you really desire. This normal state of voluntary obedience is the condition for retaining the capitalist mode of production.

7.
The Flesh of Democracy

A DAZZLING GIRL STRUTS down the catwalk like a model. The bright light reflects her on the screen, but audiences cannot recognize her, only seeing her silhouette. After the short runway show in darkness, interviewers ask her whether she is the very person whom they expect to meet again. She delightedly answers them, "Yes, I am." They repeat the question; "Is it true?" She responds again, "Yes, I am." The head of the interview panel announces, "Well, let us see that the girl standing there is the one we saw before." Her figure is finally revealed in the light, and the sound of the audience's surprise rings out. The show culminates with everyone being happy. The girl turns out to be an applicant who had suffered from her appearance and applied for the reality TV show, which gifts the opportunity of plastic surgery to those who are unhappy with their looks.

This reality TV show is called *Let Me In* (*Let* 美人), which connotes a double meaning in Korean: first, let me live a happy life; secondly, let me be beautiful. The Chinese character 美, for "beauty," is pronounced in Korean like the word *me* in English, so the title of the show thus indicates the symptomatic reality of Korean society. As such, the title was not chosen accidentally; the implication of the title seems grotesque, or at least bizarre, but it reminds us of the common utilitarian presupposition, i.e., happiness depends on management of the quantity of pleasure. According to utilitarianism, happiness relies on the quantitative amount of pleasure; in other words, the utilitarian would say that the more pleasure you have, the happier you are. Of course, this principle might be sustainable to the extent that you are in line with justice, which requires sharing an equal part of the total happiness with other members of the community. In this sense, it is crucial for the utilitarian project to govern the distribution of pleasure equally. The management of desire is at the core of the utilitarian perspective on democracy; democracy is not the liberation of desire, instead requiring responsibility to control or achieve what is wanted.

The utilitarian imperative attached to the egalitarian distribution of desire always already presupposes a blurred boundary between aesthetics and ethics. You must enjoy your pleasure in balance. Otherwise, you risk being blamed. Jacques Rancière's discussion of the relation between aesthetics and ethics serves to highlight how aesthetics is integrated with ethics. According to him, aesthetics is "a delimitation of spaces and times, of the visible and the invisible, speech and noise, which simultaneously determines the place and the stakes of politics as a form of experience."[1] The distribution of the sensible constitutes the regime of aesthetics as it regards the ethics of the community; in other words, the ethical dimension always resides in the distribution of pleasure. Indeed, aesthetics is the way in which any community necessarily shares happiness. The connection between aesthetics and ethics serves as the foundation for the modern pleasure principle and gives birth to the principle of equality.

From this perspective, it is not difficult to see that *Let Me In* also follows this principle. Ironically, the motto of this show, which is suggested in the beginning, is "Let the beauty out from inside of you." This perfectly describes the dialectic of desire. I have conceptualized this aspect of Korean popular culture as the egalitarianism of pleasure, which is relevant to the principle of equality. Whatever it once represented, it represents the equality of pleasure, i.e., the idea that all desire is equal so long as it does not infringe upon the enjoyment of others. Therefore, the egalitarianism of pleasure is the result of subtraction. What must be subtracted from a good or healthy desire is a bad or ill desire, i.e., *jouissance*. The egalitarianism of pleasure is an axiomatic rule to enforce the equal state of the individuals in the community, the state that has already eliminated the very singularity of *jouissance*. In this way, *Let Me In*, the Korean reality TV show, insinuates the truth of Korean society, the truth that the neoliberal materialism of human capital has become the dominant norm of life. The show is the site where beauty becomes the natural source of human capital in the new model of capitalist accumulation.

Around four decades ago, liberal economists such as Theodore Schultz, Gary Becker, and Jacob Mincer invented a human capital theory to justify the novel aspect of postindustrial capitalism. The theory of human capital adapts complicated mathematical formulas to prove the possibility of human capital. Its general goal is to show that investment in human capital could have a more profitable return. Although the concept of human capital needs rigorous mathematical proof to estimate the return on investment, it is already familiar to daily public debates. Human capital is nothing less than a buzzword in our lives. The flourishing of the self-help industry proves that the theory of human capital no longer remains within the boundaries of academia, having already spread to the market. The self-help industry is a vast industry that floods bookstores as well as convention centers. The industry produces its own celebrities out of ordinary people and colonizes the unconscious of recent generations. It is imperative to develop your human capital, otherwise you will lose out. South Korea is not exceptional in this regard. *Let Me In* resides within the very logic of the self-help industry.

As a mode of production, postindustrial capitalism contrasts sharply with industrial capitalism in its understanding of labor power. In industrial capitalism, according to the theory of human capital, the measure of economic value supports the idea that all labor power is equal. This idea is the basis for the measure of labor.

The concept of human capital stands against this idea, recognizing the uneven quality of labor power, and investment to improve an employee's quality is necessary for productivity. A worker's education, experience and abilities should account for their economic value for the entire financial context as well as for the employer. The most common way to accumulate human capital is through education. According to the theorists who support the human capital theory with mathematical data, education has priority for enhancing a worker's skill level and, thereby, their human capital. A higher degree of skill in terms of labor power increases the capacity for production.

In South Korea, the rapid progress of industrialization between the mid-1960s and the late 1970s catalyzed easy access to higher education in order to fulfill labor market demand for skillful workers. This economic growth pressure explains why the national passion for economic development became welded to Korean educational fever. In those days, national economic developmentalism designed a model of national modernization led by a strong government. The idea of national economic development has survived to this day, but this has only occurred through the idea of self-development. The educational fever driven by the imperative of national economic growth now instigates the passion for better managing one's appearance in the interest of human capital.

The Ideology of Plastic Surgery

The human capital theory is the new version of neoclassical economics, which Pierre Bourdieu bluntly criticizes as a myth. For Bourdieu, the mathematical formulation of economics can justify itself in the way that it allows neoclassical economists to separate economic logic from the social and historical conditions in which it comes to exist. The use of simple mathematical models and the simulated testing of hypotheses postulate the experimental method, but they cannot obtain universal conclusions. They are explicitly comprehensible as being historical, and the simplified economic models are not able to approach historical realities. To some extent, Bourdieu's criticism of economic models is straightforward and functional. Yet whatever the criticism proposes, the economic models succeed in justifying the new norm of life in postindustrial or, if you prefer, late capitalism.

Let Me In is an example that testifies to the ways that economic models imbue the mind with the neoliberal materialism of human capital. There is no single definition of neoliberalism. It is not difficult to find many approaches to its effects; however, a view mostly shared is that it has caused a paradigm shift in the meaning of life. Michel Foucault first attempted to scrutinize the origin of neoliberalism and its significant impact on everyday life. Sometimes, his analysis seems to stay at the level of description and is not fully developed, but his genealogical approach to the transformation of liberal governmentality is insightful. As Foucault analyzes, neoliberal governmentality stresses the natural principle of competition among individuals for economic evolution.

According to Foucault, disciplinary power and biopower are the modern forms of power distinguished from sovereign power. While sovereign power exercises the right to either take life or let live, disciplinary power and biopower presuppose the liberty or freedom of the individual. These two forms of power stand for the modernized way of dealing with life since the eighteenth century. Furthermore, biopower is different from disciplinary power in that the former focuses on the population rather than the individual body, even though it frequently intersects with discipline. If disciplinary power restricts the individual body with rules, biopower operates on the norms of living. The latter power aims at the administration of life. What is required to control life through biopower is a new way of governing, the art of governance founded on the idea of "corporal liberty" as seen in the arguments of

Thomas Hobbes. In this sense, liberalism can be understood as the theoretical construction of modernity.

Liberalism is the general framework for biopolitics and the governmental art of life justified by the role of liberty, i.e., "the principle of the self-limitation of governmental reason."[2] Biopower as the form of regulatory power gives rise to biopolitics, whose aim is to control the population and whose tactics are the practices of demographers, sociologists, and economists. As biopolitics is the problem of population, which is the basis of political economy, liberalism is always related to the economy rather than to politics. From this perspective, governance in the liberalist criterion should be limited to the question of economic truth and tailored to economic efficiency. Thus, utility is considered most crucial for the purpose of governance. This axiom of liberalism is not consistent with raison d'état, the "rationalization of practice, which places itself between a state presented as given and a state presented as having to be constructed and built."[3]

Originally, the art of governance required the stabilization of rules and the rationalization of the state's objective. In this way, the task of governance was identical to what the state should be. As Foucault says, before the advent of liberalist governmentality, the purpose of governance was to maximize the state as much as it could consider or calculate. The rationale was to appeal to the stable, wealthy, and permanent state. However, liberalism is clearly opposed to this premise. What is at stake in the liberalist art of governance is the way to limit governmental reason to economic truth, so to speak, the truth of the free market. With this shift, politics becomes the means to theorize relations among governmental institutions, resorting to a new way in which discipline and biopower act on the individual body and populations regarding preventive immunization. It is likely that biopolitics is concerned with the population as a set of political and scientific problems under the regime of liberalism, constituting a different condition of knowledge about *bios*.

Liberalism tends to praise limited government, governing less while maximizing effectiveness, because its principles were founded upon two levels of biopower—discipline and biopolitics. Biopower aims at knowledge/power through the practice of academic expertise. Science as knowledge/power plays a crucial role in operating biopower over the individual body and populations. In this sense, the rise of liberalism seems to dovetail with that of Social Darwinism and eugenics, one of its derivative theories. Chloë Taylor argues:

> Social Darwinism and eugenics may be depicted as biopolitical movements since they involve strategies for managing the health and productivity of populations through interventions in natality and mortality rates, mental and physical health, and immigration, even if what is taken to be "healthy" is highly problematic, entailing as it does prejudices ranging from ableism and classism to sexism, nationalism and racism ... Eugenic uses of science also arguably continue in the cases of pro-family financial, social and political incentives, designer babies, genetic counselling, preemptive abortions, and the creation of "genius sperm banks." Many of these examples entail the use of new scientific technology to improve the genes of individual babies and of the population as a whole while preventing babies deemed "unfit" from ever being born. These biopolitical practices thus further entrench the prejudices of an ableist society while continuing the goals of eugenics in manners which have become increasingly unbounded by the state.[4]

Taylor's argument reveals that the foundation of biopolitics lies in Social Darwinism. The idea of competition, which is a variation of Herbert Spencer's Social Darwinism, is an abstractive machine to justify the market system as the natural condition for survival. The nature of the market incites the individual to struggle to be the fittest, i.e., competition; otherwise, they will perish according to the natural law of evolution. The idea of competition emerges with the new norms of life in the "postwar" phase of capitalism imposed on non-Western countries regarding modernization. South Korea is one of the most prosperous countries, having adhered to US postwar capitalist policy. The anticommunist ideology of the Cold War functions in Asian countries as disciplinary regulation to produce the modern body for the international division of labor. Authoritarian state power played a pivotal role in implementing the law of competition for the modern body. Rampant educational fever swept the nation during intense economic development. For this reason, the process of Korean modernization would be an example that explains how "postwar" liberalism already presumed interventionism and paved the way toward neoliberalism.

Based on authoritarian governmentality, the nation built by the postwar liberal project became a neoliberal machine that internalized the self-governance ideology of biopolitics. This historical process is significant for understanding the popularity of reality TV shows like *Let Me In* and the neoliberalization of the human body that comes with the principle of competition and ends with the extreme materialism of "corporal liberty."

With this consideration of the lineage shared by liberalism and neoliberalism, we can understand why the idea of neoliberal self-governance brings forth a widespread obsession with the way in which a worker must increase their human capital. The normative notion of human capital for a better life, the idea that an individual worker should be productive like Steve Jobs, comes to be adopted firmly as an ethical standard. According to this rule, the individual must prove that their value can be equally exchangeable with the market value, and the human body, the very embodiment of *bios*, is regarded as the potential productivity for capitalist accumulation.

The hidden impetus behind the obsession with plastic surgery is nothing more than the desire to look attractive because good looks are a crucial advantage for finding a good job in South Korea. This condition drives people to believe that landing a good job requires a better opportunity to accumulate human capital. As Matt Stiles reported, "Facing intense competition for jobs with benefits, many applicants feel compelled to enhance their appearances for an edge,"[5] with some naturally resorting to dermatology or plastic surgery. According to the report, a job blog advises prospective applicants that "big firms prefer 'pretty eyes' and that government bosses like 'high noses.'"[6] This explains why a TV program like *Let Me In* should be considered symptomatic of neoliberal body politics.

With hyper-competition for jobs, the ocular-centrism of "lookism" constitutes the core of the ideological consensus that all people must develop their value by managing their corporality. Appearance becomes a central issue in competition, even though everyone has already gained the sufficient qualifications to find a job. Appearance is the essence here with this depthless materialism. More importantly, the growing emphasis on everyday appearance turns ugliness into a form of social disability. In this way, the ideology of plastic surgery resides in precisely the way in which neoliberal state apparatuses reproduce the subjectivity of the working class. Furthermore, the strategy of reproduction is to remove class consciousness from the worker in capitalism in order to finally reach the utopia of liberalism, i.e., capitalism without a working class.

In this sense, the widespread use of the term *plastic surgery*, rather than *cosmetic surgery*, seems symptomatic because *plastic surgery* seems intended to cancel the guilty feeling of lust that saturates the term *cosmetic surgery*. The term *cosmetic surgery* implies an excessive desire for beauty, and any excess is dangerous with respect to utilitarianism. Lust, the excessive passion for enjoyment, would destroy the egalitarian order of pleasure. However, the term *plastic surgery* seems to reduce such a burden of lust. Suppose you say, "I should have plastic surgery" rather than "cosmetic surgery." In this case, it sounds like you are committed to something necessary and important for a better life due to the new norm of life, the norm that an individual has a responsibility to enhance their human capital.

The Korean situation reveals the essence of capitalist materialism as such, which totalizes differences like body and soul into an integrated unity. Such capitalist materialism is nothing less than the imposition of equality among differences—individuals should regard themselves as equal entities. What is this kind of materialism? In *Logics of Worlds*, Alain Badiou clarified a key methodological distinction between dialectical materialism and "democratic materialism," the materialism that verifies the axiom of conviction on bodies and languages only without truths. The problem is thinking, not desire as such.

Biopolitics in Asia

Let Me In demonstrates how the neoliberal idea of self-development controls "corporal liberty" and goes beyond the limit of liberalism. On passing its critical point, it is revealed that the utilitarian ideal of happiness falls into crisis from within. There arises a paradox when everyone tries to achieve each happiness. For the solution to this paradox, the theory of competition must be introduced to manage the democratic principle of equality. Social Darwinism was the theoretical source that supports the theory of competition. In this sense, the theory of human capital would be the contemporary variation of Social Darwinism.

Dating back to the early twentieth century, the liberalism introduced into the Asian context went hand in hand with Social Darwinism. Historically, Japan was the first country to import Social Darwinism. Japanese scholars translated European Social Darwinian texts, including Herbert Spencer and Thomas Huxley. From 1877, Edward Morse, an American biologist, taught zoology at Tokyo University. Morse was a correspondent with Darwin and one of the first people to introduce Social Darwinism to Japan. He was mainly interested in the evolutionary approach to zoology but also occasionally applied his scientific research to understanding Japanese history. In line with his Darwinian perspective, he audaciously argued that ancient Japanese history was "a series of violent conquests of the 'unfit' by the 'fitter,'" an argument that "neatly matched the popularized model of Social Darwinism."[7]

Social Darwinism was transformed into a theory to justify Japanese self-confidence in imperialism when the country invented its official ideology by combining Shintoism with Confucianism in the 1890s. The evolution of species served as a theoretical category that was simply compatible with social progress. Above all, such an evolutionary theory mirrored the new science then explaining the world in a modern way. Social Darwinists described the world as a jungle where the struggle of species to be the fittest constituted life as such. Scientific knowledge of biological life seemed to guarantee the way in which Japan could be the "fittest country" for survival in the competition of nations. In this sense, for those who desired modernization, the central concept that Social Darwinism vitalized was the competition for survival. The presence of Darwinism dramatically led to the most influential position in the Korean context. It was Yu Kiljun, a young Korean student, who first encountered Social Darwinism. He was sent to Japan in 1881, partly for a Korean Courtiers' observation mission and partly for study. While in Tokyo, he attended Morse's lecture and was fascinated by his teachings. After his return to Korea two years later, Yu wrote a short treatise about his understanding of Social Darwinism, entitled "The Theory of Competition." To quote,

> Among all the affairs of human life, it is impossible to find any that does not rely on competition. From the affairs of world's states down to the affairs of one's household – everything progresses due to competition. Were there no competition in human lives, how could wisdom, virtues and happiness be advanced? If the states did not compete with each other, how could they increase their strength, wealth, and prestige? Generally, competition starts with personal cultivation of wisdom and virtue and then reaches literature, crafts, and all manners of agriculture and commerce. Everybody compares one's achievements to those of others and wishes to surpass them … Generally speaking, dull-witted men and women tend to barely avoid cold and hunger. Because they simply sleep and eat, without making a single effort to advance themselves and knowing nothing about self-cultivation, they are doomed to live and die in poverty and stupidity. The only reason for this is their ultimate lack of competitive spirit … At the same time, gentlemen of great ambition and wisdom daily cultivate their intelligence and virtue and improve their skills, thus contributing to the world, advancing their occupations and bringing prestige and happiness to their families. Those who are useful to the states under heaven are necessarily those with strong and lofty competitive spirit.[8]

Yu regarded competition as a necessary virtue for human beings, their ability for self-cultivation over poverty and stupidity. It is not difficult to see the nascent idea of biopolitics in his discussion of competition. Meanwhile, his terminology is impressive in the sense that he put an emphasis on subjectivity, using "strong and lofty competitive spirit." For him, modern subjectivity is necessary to build a new nation. In this way, the idea of biopolitics, including discipline, was influential in Yu's understanding of Social Darwinism. The similarity between Yu's argument and liberal biopolitics is not accidental. Social Darwinism lent theoretical support to the liberal idea that individual liberty must be bolstered by free economic activity, particularly competition in a free market. Liberalism, which gradually emerged in the seventeenth and eighteenth centuries, was in its origin nothing less than a new way to discipline life according to economic rules and theorization regarding the limits of government. The market became the place of truth under the theoretical umbrella of liberalism; that is to say, the locus of the law of natural selection. The fittest must have survived against the competitive surroundings.

At the time Yu wrote "The Theory of Competition," the idea of competition adopted by liberalism was crucial for Asian politics. It would lead to a paradigm shift in the understanding of social problems. For instance, it had been believed that poverty was caused by vicious rulers who failed to govern people. In light of the liberalist idea welded with Social Darwinism, people started to believe that poverty was merely the consequence of personal failure. Poverty is the by-product of the competitive process; the natural law of the free market gives rise to inferiority since some lose the game. In this respect, liberal governance is framed by integrated natural laws—the laws make men what they are in the natural state of the economy. Yu's understanding of Social Darwinism was compatible with liberal biopolitics and had the effect of criticizing the powerless Korean monarchy. Still, he was not interested in the democratic mechanism of modernization. What attracted him was the law of social evolution, which could be analogous to the natural selection of species. From this perspective, Yu regarded international relations as a natural, competitive environment in which the fittest survive. Here, competition, the fundamental cause of superiority, turns the wheel of history by imposing the necessity of evolution on the human species. For him, the decline of the Korean monarchy was the necessary result of the irresistible process.

The problem with Yu's viewpoint, regardless of his conflation of nature and society, is that there is no place for subjectivity in history if the historical transformation is merely the realization of evolutionary law. The materialistic framework of Social Darwinism illustrates how to properly manage an individual life from top to bottom, ignoring social relations in the mode of production. Indeed, it is unsurprising that the political consequence of such an intellectual inclination resulted in Yu's approval for Japan's colonization of Korea. The stronger nation should win the international competition against the weaker one by evolutionary necessity. Yu's attitude toward imperialism as the highest evolutionary stage of the nation-state might result from his understanding of competition as the natural law ingrained within the normative value of life. According to this logic, the crucial element for governance is to make individuals natural.

The reception of Social Darwinism in China was even more remarkable than this. Yan Fu, a Chinese translator of John Stuart Mill, Thomas Huxley, and Herbert Spencer known as one of the pioneering scholars to have introduced liberalism to China, delivered a public lecture on politics on October 13, 1905. What he emphasized during the presentation was that politics is nothing less than the science of governmentality for the production of a better nation-state; he distinguished science from technology and was convinced that through understanding the scientific laws of history correctly, the Chinese could survive political turbulence. His lecture had one of the most notable broad impacts on the Asian intellectual milieu, as well as on China's own.

Yan Fu's lecture was concerned with the scientific theory of politics but showed a way to view liberalism through the lens of Social Darwinism. His translation of Mill revealed his understanding of liberalism interwoven with Spencer's social evolution theory. To quote Hao Chang,

> Yen [Yan] was interested in the Western value of vitality and struggle because, in his view, these values were key to the wealth and power of Western nations. By the same token, Yen [Yan] was led to believe that the lack of these animating values in the Chinese tradition accounted for the weakness of China.[9]

Like Yu, Yan Fu also discovered the normative value of competition in liberalism. Due to Yan Fu's attempt to disseminate the idea of competition throughout the Chinese intellectual scene, Social Darwinism formed the center of an emerging national identity that incorporated the imaginary of the community, deeply rooted in a hierarchical culture based on family lineage. Such a transformation revolves around the application of selection to culture and society. The logical process is not merely the application of biological concepts of general selection for super-biotic entities but rather the production of knowledge on the variation, selection, and retention of autonomous cultural bodies. By reconstructing a way of thinking, the concept of nation quickly becomes a category in which the identity of the community, the logical basis that constitutes "us," excludes "not us" from membership.

Biopolitics has functioned alongside Social Darwinism—or better still, progressivism—in Asian countries, including in South Korea. Such a political combination has suggested an "ideal community of citizens" different from what the West presupposed. The imagination stemming from Asian biopolitics is concerned not with the citizens as the ideal people but with the population as the entities of life, which are reduced to the labor power that comprises the force of production. Is this correct if one argues that Asian modernization is unique, therefore suggesting that nothing can be universal? To a certain point, it would be right, but some authoritarian politicians and dictators—for instance, Park Chung Hee in South Korea, Kim Jeong Il in North Korea, and Lee Gwang Yo in Singapore—have argued that "our" Asian modernity is incomprehensible and cannot be explained by Western criteria. However, what is at stake is that the Asian historical context, in which Social Darwinism played a key role, proves the possibility of modernization without liberalism and politics without citizens. Asian modernization reveals the self-contradiction of liberal governmentality, the contradiction within its civility and its biopolitics, and the crisis of liberalism independent of the capitalist economy that Foucault clearly points out.

The Failure of Law

Social theories influenced by Darwinism criticized the utilitarian solution to the management of desire and emphasized the intrinsic nature of human beings. According to these theories, the law of evolution rules over society and everyone must obey the law if the nation is to progress. Otherwise, humanity will regress and soon be extinct. Although the evolutionary rule is called natural law, it means economic determinism, wherein the economy is the foundation of human life, and everything in society should be subordinate to the growth of material necessities. From this perspective, the individual is the ultimate entity to sustain the ongoing evolution. In this way, the stigma of *homo economicus*, the idea of self-governing subjectivity, fosters the belief that only the strongest survive competition. Eugenics was the extreme version of social evolutionism; the winner of this evolutionary contest was the strongest.

The perverse adaptation of the Darwinian imperative, i.e., the fittest wins, became dominant after the failure of liberalism. Defenders would argue that the Darwinian idea of the fittest has nothing to do with a eugenic imagination. However, Spencer coined the notion and handed it over to Darwin. Spencer developed the idea that evolution is the process that leads from the simple, indefinite, and incoherent to the complex, definite, and coherent. Therefore, whatever Darwin intended, Spencer's conceptualization of the fittest does not seem free from what Social Darwinism argues.

The imperative to be the strongest was crucial for nation-building in the early twentieth century in Asia, but it is now, in the twenty-first century, compulsory for the development of perfect human capital. The idea of the winner amid international competition was the capitalist *raison d'état* for the nation-state and is today the capitalist *raison d'état* for the individual. This shift could be called the neoliberal transformation, which encourages a hedonistic solution to social inequality. In this way, social problems suddenly turn into personal affairs: the party responsible for solving the issues is not supposed to be government or society but the individual who faces up to them. Neoliberal egalitarianism is built on the principle that human capital depends on the individual's capacity to manage their own desires. This egalitarianism paradoxically bases itself in justification of the inequality between winners and losers in market competition, between those who are the fittest and those who are the most unfit for capitalism.

Meanwhile, the theory of human capital is one variation of the evolutionary imagination that embraced Social Darwinism in the early twentieth century. The evolutionary law still plays a crucial role in constructing neoliberal egalitarianism. The law seems to prohibit excessive desires that would impede the accumulation of human capital. If you want to be a winner, you must tailor your desire to the capitalist market. Otherwise, you will become extinct through competition. Neoliberal egalitarianism is another facet of the pleasure principle—the modern imperative to enjoy yourself. For this reason, one must pretend to enjoy oneself, even though we cannot do that. Self-enjoyment is the energy source for capitalist consumerism, and "enjoy yourself" is the order of the unconscious, always excessive but less than nothing.

As *Let Me In* proves, the law of neoliberal egalitarianism cannot be self-fulfilling. The law of self-enjoyment is not omnipotent but impotent. The pleasure principle strives to hide the truth, i.e., the lack of the Other. There is no such law that prohibits our desire, and we instead forbid ourselves from knowing this. In this sense, desire is not merely gratified with its objects. This is the reason why utilitarian hedonism fails to achieve its goals. Desire is not a well-organized room but one in which some chairs have always already fallen over. It arises from a novel situation where the desired event breaks down and fails. Desire is not uniform but singular on different levels. The passion for plastic surgery in South Korea exhibits the ultimate stance of biopolitics combined with the theory of human capital, yet it also proves that the neoliberal egalitarianism of pleasure is impossible.

8.
Hegel and Netflix

THE COVID-19 PANDEMIC does not mean the crisis of capitalism; it instead compounds the existing problems within the capitalist mode of production. The precarious status of essential workers, regardless of their living conditions, has worsened. By contrast, unrestricted capitalist accumulation has, by valorizing the market above all else, both become more efficient and exacerbated social inequality. These contradictory consequences of the pandemic prove that the nature of capitalism does not need workers for its completion. The pandemic serves not so much as the end of capitalism but as another moment through which to sustain its paradox. Indeed, what can presently be observed is the more traumatic experience of capitalist restructuring. Some critics have used the concept of the "shock doctrine" to explain how capitalism survives through the process of disaster. Naomi Klein's theory of the shock doctrine, her critique of the Chicago School, assumes that "the human cost of shock therapy" is tactically designed to control the working class.[1] The basis of the shock doctrine is undoubtedly the human's psychical realm, and it essentially requires production's social relations. The current prevalence of disaster capitalism seems to reach its culmination by erasing the presence of the working class. However, this means not the removal of workers but the modification of work as such.

This transformation led dramatically, during the pandemic, to the idea of mechanical management based on surveillance technology. In other words, the mechanization of work, the perversion of Taylorism, reconstructs the labor force's fundamentals and drives each worker to be a part of the mechanism. The financial bull market on investment in technology precipitates this shift further and reformulates the distribution of labor. I would call this inversion of capitalism the very essence of "pure capitalism," i.e., the "free" economic system that encourages individuals' voluntary competition to produce and trade without government intervention. It is not easy to determine where administrative interference could engage the system if workers have no human management. "My Boss Is Not Human" (我的领导不是人), an article recently published in *Caijing*, a Chinese economic magazine, proves how this mechanical surveillance reorganizes the workplace.[2]

According to the report, many Chinese enterprises have adopted artificial intelligence for standardized and more efficient management. The new system works with more than 20 surveillance cameras throughout the workplace and records each worker's behavior and activity. An electronic roll call at the entrance is necessary to identify each person and monitor the group. This algorithmic scrutiny, the mechanical transformation of all human action into data, totalizes the entire process of work like a single machine. The monitoring camera transcribes worker performance by the second, and the central operating system checks efficiency. Each component is assigned a prescribed processing time by the algorithm, and the Intelligent Task Distribution System recognizes and facilitates the worker's actions. The electronic time attendance system refines the check-in procedures previously set at the company gate. Workers must swipe their cards if they leave the workplace. If they are absent from their seats for more than 15 minutes, the recorded data will be submitted to the central operating system and the appropriate sum will be automatically deducted from the worker's salary at the end of the month.

My point concerning this Chinese version of Taylor's scientific management lies not in the fact that Orwell's imagination of Big Brother has come to be realized but in the fact that the administration's aim is to modify human behavior for the algorithmic mechanism. There is no such thing as Big Brother within the system, only the technological stupidity of controlling workers by simplifying their actions. Any digressive or unforeseen move does not seem to be allowed in this process. However, the workers follow the rules not because the system tightly governs them but because the norm of the new scientific management, i.e., the command of the mechanical surveillance, forces them to obey the axioms of the mechanism. The algorithmic organization of the workplace is therefore not a crucial factor in the new management. The problem is that there must be an invisible decision-maker behind the automatic system to solve any accidental and unpredictable outcomes, even though the algorithmic mechanism operates without the presence of a human boss in the venue. The void of the surveillance, i.e., the subjective articulation, is always already included in the mechanism and preserves the locus of resistance. My experience with Netflix during the pandemic suggests an example to justify this assumption.

Algorithm and Choice

Recently, I watched two films: *Love per Square Foot* (2018) and *Leap Year* (2010). The former was made in Bollywood, and the latter in Hollywood. Interestingly, I discovered opposing messages in these different products. *Love per Square Foot* displays the young Indian middle class's wish fulfillment, while *Leap Year* presents the American middle class's disillusionment with life. The Indian movie is about an Indian boy, Sanjay Chaturvedi, and an Indian girl, Karina D'souza, who work for the same bank. Sanjay is an IT engineer, and Karina is a bank cashier. They each have dreams of owning their own "house," but these dreams are constantly interrupted by their personal lives. Sanjay has an affair with his boss, Rashi Khurana, who refuses to leave her husband, while Karina is engaged to her boyfriend and has a mother who thwarts her dream of owning a house. However, everything starts to change when Sanjay finds out about a joint housing scheme, which is supposed to provide an available apartment to a newly married couple. He suggests to Karina that they apply for it together, and she agrees to his plan to lie to the authorities and get married.

Meanwhile, *Leap Year* follows the journey of Anna Brady, a real estate worker who is heading to Dublin to propose to her boyfriend, Jeremy, on a leap day. According to Irish tradition, on the date of February 29, men cannot reject a woman's proposal for marriage. While Anna and her boyfriend live together in Boston, he has not yet proposed to her. His hesitation inspires her decision to embark on the adventure. On the road to Dublin, she meets an Irishman, Declan O'Callaghan, who is an innkeeper and chef. Because there is no public transportation, she desperately asks Declan to drive her to Jeremy's place. Of course, as is typical in romantic comedies, Anna and Declan gradually discover their mysterious attachment to each other, even though Declan keeps complicating things. After many twists and turns, they finally arrive at the hotel, where, surprisingly, Jeremy proposes to Anna. However, Jeremy's intention is far from Anna's dream. At the engagement party in Boston, Anna learns that Jeremy's marriage proposal was merely to satisfy the co-op board of the apartment building they want to buy into (the board's unspoken rule is that only married couples can move into the property together). Disappointed, Anna leaves Jeremy and goes back to Ireland to confirm her true love for Declan.

Interestingly, these two films deal with marriage and housing—the material foundation of the middle class, so to speak—in quite opposite ways. For the Indian couple, housing is the necessary fulfillment of their love, while the American heroine believes property to symbolize fake love and decides to give it up for true love. One could simply explain this gap as the consequence of different cultural values, yet there seems to be a more serious ideological distinction in these representations of the middle class. This difference reveals that the Indian imaginary representation of middle-class life is the imitation of American liberalism, not a more in-depth self-orientation from within. Symptomatically, *Love per Square Foot* erases the Indian reality of inequality and propagates the neoliberal imperative to manage oneself for well-being. In the last scene of the film, Sanjay, who has successfully accomplished his mission, discovers another boy standing on the rooftop of his shabby house. They make eye contact, and Sanjay smiles to the young man as if he is the mirror image of himself from a few months prior. The gaze of the interactive observation is the principal component of surveillance that sustains the new spirit of capitalism.

On the contrary, *Leap Year* rails against the fantasy of the American middle-class life. Anna has no real life, and her job is to "stage" empty houses for sale. This figure of the heroine is an image of the typical modernist critique of the hollow life. The Indian romantic comedy lacks this element of modernism. All the conflicting differences that revolve around the narrative ultimately reconcile with the whole Indian community through the dialectical process. Despite its standard genre cliches, *Love per Square Foot* is not a romantic drama but a postartistic reproduction of the romantic comedy in the Hegelian sense. Ironically, the movie marks the end of a romantic relationship. It would be affirmed that this postartistic tendency springs from recent developments in the Bollywood style: the rebranding of the Hollywood genre with Indian aesthetics, which is widely observable in non-Western films. But what about *Leap Year*? The movie seems to praise the individual right of self-determination lightly affected by feminism while criticizing capitalist consumerism and the neoliberal ethos of efficiency. However, its modernist gestures result in the utilitarian morality of marriage, concluding that true love must lead to the legal form of family planning. I do not intend here to bring forth a comparative study of Bollywood and Hollywood; suffice it to say that I watched two different films accidentally during lockdown.

I happened to discover these films on Netflix, encountering *Love per Square Foot* first and *Leap Year* second. I didn't "intend" to watch the two movies one after another. It was Netflix that led me to *Leap Year* after I had watched *Love per Square Foot*. This recommendation would have been programmed in Netflix's algorithm. In other words, my taste in movie selection was read by the new tele-technology of mechanical categorization. Without this technology, I could not have watched the two films consecutively, or at least had a comparative understanding of them. The contingency of the empirical moment occurred in my experience of two movies via artificial intelligence. Without any doubt, it was "me" who selected and decided to watch the second movie by checking Netflix's list of recommendation, but it was not "my purpose" that brought me to the choice and decision. Even the hesitation in taking more time to decide for my pleasure does not belong to the machine. The logic of Netflix relies heavily on arbitrary choices. That feeling of reluctance makes us believe that "we can choose" or that "we have a will to select."

Teleology vs Mechanism

Netflix is a mechanism that seems to have no purpose determined by external intelligence. It lacks intelligence despite being considered an example of artificial intelligence, and it confuses us with deferred moments of choice, functioning as though our selections have a purpose. This mechanism not only aggregates massive amounts of random data but also turns it into essential business intelligence. Hegel had already anticipated the advent of Netflix in his discussion, half in jest, of the distinction between mechanism and teleology. In *The Science of Logic*, Hegel argued that "where there is the perception of a *purposiveness*, an *intelligence* is assumed as its author; required for purpose is thus the concept's own free concrete existence." He continues:

> *Teleology* is above all contrasted with *mechanism*, in which the determinateness posited in the object, being external, is one that gives no sign of *self-determination*. The opposition between *causæ efficientes* and *causæ finales*, between merely *efficient* and *final causes*, refers to this distinction, just as, at a more concrete level, the enquiry whether the absolute essence of the world is to be conceived as blind mechanism or as an intelligence that determines itself in accordance with purposes also comes down to it.[3]

Fatalism is opposed to freedom, and this opposition can be applied to the opposition between mechanism and teleology. Freedom is only possible in its concrete existence. In this sense, a mechanism is grounded in the immediacy of objectivity. This objective immediacy is the stupidity of Netflix. The algorithm based upon big data shapes our preference of choice. This rule does not allow us any "freedom" to take different actions. This iron cage of the tele-technological mechanism is the principle of platform media amid the context of the pandemic. Algorithmic machines, such as Netflix, YouTube, and Facebook, tame our taste for objects and serve as the possible formation of the present actuality. Ironically, when technology reduces our lives to measurable data points, we begin to view our existence itself as mechanical. Hegel's use of teleology will be considered here in order to reinstate the "purpose" of technology against the mechanization of life.

According to Hegel, the objective moments "stand in self-subsistent indifference as *objects each outside the other*, and as so related they possess the *subjective unity* of the concept only as *inner* or as *outer*."[4] Meanwhile, when the essential unity of the objects is posited as "distinct from their self-subsistence" and its concept is subjective but presumed to be "referring in and for itself to the objectivity, as *purpose*," it is teleology. Hegel continues to claim that "since purpose is the concept posited as within it referring to objectivity, and through itself sublating its defect of being subjective, the at first *external* purposiveness becomes, through the realization of the purpose, *internal*."[5] This argument clarifies how purpose becomes an *idea*.

Hegel's teleology separates his idealism from other idealists—Berkeley and Kant, in particular, who regard mind and rational subjectivity as the origin of objects. For Hegel, neither spiritual nor ideal elements (which go beyond Kant's concept of self-consciousness) exist at the start of thought and being. Rather, they emerge only at the conclusion of these developmental processes. Hegel's spiritualism presupposes the traumatic "education" of spirituality extracted from the defects and errors of subjectivity. In this sense, Hegel's teleology allows us to think beyond the necessity of mechanisms like Netflix. Ironically, the purpose of the technology lies in the flaw of its mechanism, i.e., the subjective hesitation, our reluctant pause before our choice. In other words, there is no final decision there, only indecision, which has no absolute other from outside but rather deferring differences from within. The Hegelian use of teleology aims at bringing a metalogical approach to the automatic algorithm.

Resistance within Mechanisms

In my opinion, Hegel's conception of teleology can be understood as the early consideration of today's automatization. An algorithmic categorization such as Netflix reveals how mechanical necessity conceals the internalized purpose. Even though the mechanism seems automatic, there must be a hesitating decision-maker behind the machine. When the Gulf War broke out in 1990, Félix Guattari wrote an essay, "Towards A Postmedia Era," in which he posited potential resistance to the mechanical categorization of media. He pondered the images of warfare on television and stated that the images made us lift off into "an almost delirious universe of mass-media subjectivity."[6] He argued,

> The growing power of software engineering does not necessarily lead to the power of Big Brother. In fact, it is way more cracked than it seems. It can blow up like a windshield under the impact of molecular alternative practices.[7]

What are the "molecular alternative practices" of media? In a Hegelian sense, they would be possible with the creation of purpose in the use of technology. For Guattari, "postmedia" practices must constitute an expressive mediation against the mechanical representation of reality, since the good old days of media only existed in the scientific and positivist imaginary. There is no powerful Big Brother in the new tele-technological setting, but much potential resistance exists within them. In this sense, what is urgently needed is the invention of "purpose" for postmedia; in other words, a concept of postmedia that stands in and for itself. The creation of self-determinate concepts is the main task of "pure metaphysics" about "pure mechanism."

Following Henri Bergson, Gilles Deleuze defines his own philosophical purpose as a pure metaphysics adequate to modern science and technology. It is not difficult to see the similarity between Deleuze's pure metaphysics and Hegel's teleology, but it is his understanding of negation that separates Deleuze from Hegel. This rejection of Hegelian negation leads Deleuze to argue that Hegel's concept of conflict is another aspect of difference.[8] In line with Deleuze, Guattari emphasizes the "minor" use of technology.

The concept of a minority implies the affirmation of difference, i.e., those that are not subsumed by the majority's generalization. The minor use of technology is nothing less than the creation of "inner purpose." My accidental encounter with two movies on Netflix and my criticism of what I watched would be one possible practice that takes up an experimental opportunity against mechanical necessity. What is to be done in disaster capitalism is to affirm the contingency within a mechanism and create the uncategorized purpose beyond the norms of algorithmic technology, which are designed to modify our behaviors according to mechanical automatization. I believe that such resistance to technological affordances and the mechanical modification of desire will be the groundless basis for politics against "pure capitalism."

9.
Street Artists in Delhi

IN AN INTERVIEW PUBLISHED in *Cahiers du cinéma* in 1995, Jacques Rancière suggested a reinterpretation of the political meaning of cinephilia. The term *cinephilia* can be traced back to the heyday of French film production in the 1910s. Rancière connects the cinephilia of the nouvelle vague, the experimental movement of French cinema in the 1950s, with the crisis of cultural legitimacy. Faced with the classical connotation of the notion, Rancière argued that the revival of cinephilia was necessary to resist the heritagization of the cinematic movement, and he criticized its artificial homogenizing tendencies against the multiplication of heterogeneous perspectives. Rancière's defense of cinephilia can be understood as the valorization of amateurism in artistic practice.

Even though Rancière did not mention the non-European dimension of cinema, it is noteworthy to mention here that cinephilia rematerialized in the Korean nouvelle vague between the late 1980s and the early 1990s. The French cinema boom that Rancière observed deeply influenced the rise of the Korean cinematic movement. In my view, the Korean reception of French cinephilia brought forth the aesthetic dimension of Korean new wave cinema, which emerged side by side with the principle of equality during the process of Korean democratization. Bong Joon-ho's *Parasite* is a recent expression of this long revolution. Rancière's conceptualization of cinephilia is firmly rooted in the fact that mass art is a key aspect of cinema. Here, technology is consistent with the main feature of mass art. Rancière puts forward the view that technology is not merely the medium of art but the milieu of artistic performance.

Before Rancière, Walter Benjamin discussed how the introduction of the machine, e.g., photography and cinema, into artistic production changed the ontological condition of an artwork. A machine as an artist, the automatic operator of the technological sensorium, preserves the invisible dimension of representation, or in Benjamin's terms, the optical unconscious. However, Benjamin hesitates to accept the artistic aspect of technology while he confirms the role of the machine in technological reproduction, which replaces the conventional concept of the artist. Benjamin views mechanical representation as traces and signs, not the redistribution of the sensible. Rancière argues that the significant aspect of Benjamin's discussion lies in the fragmented experience of technological reproduction, not in the series of mechanical reproductions. According to Rancière, what must be stressed in Benjamin's conceptualization of technological reproducibility is not the fact that specific photographs are infinitely reproducible but that "they are products of the machine age, the age of mass existence and the man of the masses; and, moreover, that these products are also ways of training contemporaries how to decipher this new lived world and orient themselves in it."[1]

The operation of mass art is linked to the "indifferentiation" of technologies, the "de-technologization of technology" in Rancière's terms. Meanwhile, Rancière turns to another aspect of technological effects, which regards the medium as a milieu. This perspective, identified in surrealism and futurism, considers the technological medium, like photography, to give rise to a new sensory world insofar as its particular use resists its generalized exercise. Distinct from these two points of view, Rancière defends his own thesis that "the idea of the medium's specificity is always an idea of mediality."[2] The technological medium, such as photography or cinema, is the technē of recording the new sensory world and the very element of its construction. Rancière's notion of technological mediality indicates the unity of three ideas: "An idea of medium, an idea of art and an idea of sensorium within which this technological apparatus carries out the performances of art."[3] In this sense, the medium is not the means to an end but what always already declares its end.

Rancière's conceptualization of the relationship between technology and art seems to grant an insightful consideration of the exercise of mass art on the street, for instance, the performance of graffiti. The birth of cinema marked a transitory moment for artistic production, which came along with the development of technology. Since the Industrial Revolution, technology has simply been designated as an instrument. However, the idea of technē always exceeds the purpose of the apparatus. Marx clearly understands that the essence of machines is unnatural. For him, machines are "products of human industry; natural material transformed into organs of the human will over nature, or of human participation in nature."[4] The artistic use of technology reveals the transgressive dimension of machines, which is sealed within their formation. I would say this excess of technology is where the amateurism of mass art takes place, and the "multiplication" of machines creates a neutralized zone between what is and what is not art.[5]

When I visited Delhi in 2020, I encountered protests against the Citizenship Amendment Act, organized by students at Jamia Millia Islamia. What impressed me was the many instances of graffiti and paintings in the street. Sometimes, the paintings parodied official images, but most were a symbolic representation of political imaginations. They delivered various messages and slogans about the meaning of the Indian constitution. Some pedestrians took pictures of the works of art as they passed by. All of the performances I witnessed at the venue had no organizer and no director. They also lacked the distinction between artist and audience, and further, between art and non-art. The audiences who enjoyed the aesthetic performance on the street seemed to represent common folk, but they nevertheless understood the artistic meaning of the messages. They simply used their mobile phones to join the cultural scene, and they sang along with the songs that the protestors performed. With technological instruments, they carried out multiple forms of participation in the protests. Is this not the ignorant use of art regarded as non-artistic? It seems to me that technology extended the exercise of artistic performance to common audiences during the political demonstrations and enhanced the aesthetic experience on the street.

My experience of the Indian protests in 2020 allows me to question Benjamin's hesitation to consider technological reproducibility as he separated the technical aspect of artistic reproduction from the aura of the artwork. For him, technological artefacts like photographs and cinema always enable the optical unconscious and need to be interpreted accordingly. This idea leads him to the presupposition that the author is a producer. In Benjamin's sense, the author as a producer is "an operating writer" who discovers situations rather than reproducing them, and an exemplary one who teaches other writers.[6] As an intellectual, according to Benjamin, the author has a feeling of solidarity with the means of production more than with the proletariat, owing to a bourgeois education. There is a fundamental gap between a specialist and a proletariat. The "New Objectivity" enabled by technology complements activist approaches when both effectively connect with audiences.[7] In this way, their orientation toward both the bourgeois class and the *destruction* of artistic tradition is revealed.

Benjamin's conceptualization of the author as a producer is the quintessential strategy of modernism. His defense of avant-garde art aims at political aesthetics in opposition to the rise of fascism. However, his tactical aesthetics are not enough to explain the political implications of mass art. The generalization of technology allows common audiences to reproduce what they experience. Unlike what Benjamin assumes, the experience reproduced by the audience is not the mere recording of the worldly sensible but is instead the testing practice of it. Sometimes, the audience's products seem more political than any author's normative message. Amateurism in artistic practice does not inherently mean lower quality, instead offering a greater sense of the experimental and the political. Benjamin recognizes how political art is possible through the recomposition of artistic apparatuses, in other words, the different uses of technē against its original purpose; yet he lacks an understanding of the neutralizing effects of technology. Amateurism must be viewed as the multiplication of apparatuses. Art's technological turn gives rise to a global scope of artistic amateurism. Far from its instrumental purpose, technology embraces artistic moments within its operation. The multiplication of apparatuses annihilates the particularity of the art, creating zones of neutralization "wherein technologies are indifferentiated and exchange their effects, where their products present a multiplicity of gazes and readings, of zones of transfer between modes of approaching objects, of the functioning of images and of the attribution of meanings."[8] The varied use of technology against its purpose, i.e., the experimental exercise of artistic reproduction, is nothing less than the political effects of amateurism. This excessive practice of apparatuses promises the revival of art against the dissolution of art in the globalized world of technological generalization. The Delhi protest in 2019 and 2020 proves how the amateurism of art turns political through the betrayal of what is perceived as art.

10.

Sartre in Asia

FOLLOWING THE TRAUMATIC EXPERIENCE of warfare, the Cold War forced Korea's intellectuals to distort the political implication of the global philosophical movements and to emphasize their empirical elements through their translations of Sartre. The ideology of the Cold War distorted Sartre's influence on the Korean intellectuals, and their reception of his philosophy was saturated with the myth of *Bildung*. For them, existentialism was regarded as a channel through which they could access the cosmopolitan ideals of the Enlightenment. Of course, the irony of national identification lay behind this passion for global intellectualism.

Nationalism provided an excuse to read Sartre, even though his philosophy must be classified as leftist thought. Existentialism was supportive of the Third World against the political polarization of the Cold War. From the nationalist perspective, existentialism showed a possible way toward the philosophy of non-Europeans. Still, at the same time, it seemed procommunist to those who agreed with the anticommunist world order. The Korean War devastated the public sphere, and the frame of the Cold War severed a nation into two peoples. Each Korea competed to command ideological hegemony in the political conflict. In this way, existentialism served as the alternative prism of intellectualism by which Koreans in the South could critique the Stalinist Koreans in the North.

Indeed, Sartre was a symbolic intellectual leading the anti-Stalinist left, and he suggested another perspective contra orthodox Marxism-Leninism. During the colonial period, Keijo

Imperial University, now Seoul National University in the capital city of the Korean Peninsula, was a shelter for Japanese Marxists, and its academic tradition of Marxism influenced many Korean students and scholars even after World War II had ended. In a sense, North Korea was a perfect laboratory for Korean Marxists in which they tried to realize Marxist theory. Drawing on the ambitions of both Lenin and Stalin to "reform humanity," the Koreans who adopted North Korea as their republic were optimistic about the victory of socialism. On the contrary, Koreans in the South had to prove their ideological justification in opposition to the overwhelming popularity of socialist demands. From this historical background, Sartre's critique of Stalinism provided those who railed against North Korea with a compelling logic to validate their anticommunism.

The context in which South Korean intellectuals received Sartre was quite the opposite of the one in which existentialism was taken as the theoretical rationale of the non-aligned movement in the Third World. For instance, Sartre was the only European philosopher attracting public attention in the Middle East. Furthermore, his engagement with the politics of the Third World changed the relationship between the West and the non-West. According to Yoav di-Capua,

> On both sides of the Mediterranean, Sartre, his intellectual circle, and their new Arab interlocutors were eager to demonstrate that, against the polarizing logic of the Cold War and the sociopolitical stagnation of Europe, decolonization could produce revolutionary societies that were as egalitarian, free, and patriotic as they were anti-imperialist and humanistic. For Europeans of the Left and colonized people of recently liberated domains, that, in a nutshell, was the promise of Third Worldism, and, far from being a provincial African,

Asian, or Arab project, it was, in a variation on the old theme of colonial universality, a promising universal counter-project of its own.[1]

Existentialism shaped the new idea of counter-universality and further paved the way toward Third Worldism for Western and non-Western intellectuals. What is this Third Worldism? It is merely the sublimation of the Cold War, the conflict between two ideological poles, the US and the USSR in particular. Many thinkers of decolonization in the Third World, such as Franz Fanon, inspired Sartre and his philosophical circle in France. Without the political movements in the former colonial countries, the mapping out of European thought would be unlike what we know today. However, it is undeniable that the non-European reception of existentialism was rooted in a deep longing for the European tradition. Even in the Middle East, the grammar of existentialism was often used to flesh out the meaning of a "new Arab man," i.e., an Arab man as a cosmopolitan citizen.

Existentialism embraced various ideological positions and furthered politically contradictory commitments: on the one hand, the philosophical movement promised non-European intellectuals a cosmopolitan vision; on the other hand, its hidden impetus was national sentiment oriented toward local identity. The Korean right wing's appropriation of existentialism was therefore not exceptional. For them, existentialism was the means to decolonize their world and create a new country in the postwar world order. Even though existentialism was a global movement, its practice was always already entrapped by the national question.

The National Question

The ambiguity of existentialism as it relates to the national question explains the dilemma of the nation-state during the Cold

War. Following the Six-Day War, the rapid collapse of Sartre's reputation in the Arab world after he signed a pro-Zionist petition proved that the honeymoon period for existentialism and nationalism could not last forever. This split owes not to existentialism but to the subject matter internalized within the logic of a particular nation-state. The crucial point here was already revealed in Rosa Luxemburg's critique of Lenin's argument on the right to national self-determination. Rosa Luxemburg indicated the discrepancy between theoretical socialism and the workers' movement, i.e., that the workers felt socialism indirectly under the influence of nationalism.[2] This was because the agenda of socialist revolution was international while the interests of workers were national. This situation seems quite similar to that which transpired with Cold War existentialism.

Therefore, the question of nationality cannot be solved merely by emphasizing the class interests of the proletariat. Class orientation already incorporates the question of the nation-state. For this reason, it is non-Marxist to presuppose the absolute right of national self-determination because the historical development of a nation-state induces such a right. Instead, its historical circumstances must be analyzed to understand the structure of nationalism. National self-determination is not self-evident. She argued,

> We should first consider the idea of a nation-state. In order to evaluate this concept accurately, it is first necessary to search for historical substance in the idea, to see what is actually hiding behind the mask … Naturally, we are not speaking here of a nationality as a specific ethnic or cultural group. Such nationality is, of course, separate and distinct from the bourgeois aspect; national peculiarities had already existed for centuries. But here we are concerned with national movements as an element of political life, with the aspirations of

> establishing a so-called nation-state; then the connection between those movements and the bourgeois era is unquestionable.³

In short, the nation-state is the modern invention of technology to govern the population, but it does not stop at the instrumental level. The political theory of governance brings the ghostly objectivity of the nation. The whole process of building a nation-state comes with the secularization and rationalization of sovereignty. Rosa Luxemburg's analysis of the nation-state aims to clarify its historical characteristics, i.e., the link between national movements and bourgeois political success. Unlike Lenin, who regarded the national question as a means for social democracy in Russia and a slogan to unite the oppressed nationalities under the name of the working class, Rosa Luxemburg would shed light on the dissensus between the national question and socialism.

Lenin's defense of self-determination was a temporary tactic, in that he could not ignore the rise of a national consciousness that resisted empires and imperialism, even agreeing with the presupposition that the nation-state is the by-product of the bourgeoisie's historic victory. Therefore, Lenin argued that "to accuse those who support freedom of self-determination, i.e., freedom to secede, of encouraging separation, is as foolish and hypocritical as accusing those who advocate freedom of divorce of encouraging the destruction of family ties."⁴ Lenin believed that the strength of a nation-state would fall away when socialism gradually gained political stability. Lenin's optimistic vision of the interaction between nationalism and socialism is not easily acceptable today. Even worse, the ascension of nationalism, which dovetailed with populism, has dismissed socialist internationalism at each historical stage.

Lenin considered nationalism as an ideological medium with which to mobilize people to configure the future of socialism. However, nationalism does not fade away, instead being revived whenever national interest overwhelms an international cause. For instance, following Lenin's presupposition, Stalin ordered the Korean Communist Party to change its name to the Workers' Party of Korea and build a nation-state because he believed that Korean decolonization required bourgeois revolution under the banner of nationalism. The urgent task of the Workers' Party of Korea, at the time the only ruling party in North Korea, was to transform the peasantry into a working class. This so-called classifization was one of the principal doctrines in North Korea's economic policy after the Korean War. North Korea's obsession with national security and its excuse that it is developing nuclear weapons to support its national right of self-determination prove that Rosa Luxemburg's national question remains unresolved. Lenin seemed to underestimate the materiality of the nation-state. The rise and fall of existentialism in the Cold War era also followed on the heels of socialism. Of course, this problem cannot merely be attributed to the failure of the leftist experiment but could be internalized in any form of internationalism. Any attempt to be international requires facing up to the national question. Let us discuss this dilemma by considering the paradox of the nation-state.

Refugee Ontology

The postwar world order meant the reconstruction of global capitalism led by the US. However, the identity of the US is to some extent ambivalent. The country plays the role of an empire while insisting on its national interests. Its domestic politics affirms national identity while global security sustains the country as a new empire in postwar politics. The anticommunism of the Cold War was, in this sense, a strategic ideology to bridge the gap between nation-state and empire vis-à-vis the identity of the US. In my opinion, Cold War politics after the Korean War was an international project to bring forth a nation-state in the colonized countries.

Above all, Woodrow Wilson's liberal internationalism, an anticommunist response to Lenin's idea of national self-determination, successfully roused national movements in some Asian countries. Korea was one of those places where the early bourgeois nationalists discovered in Wilson's concept of self-determination the logical justification for their movements. The early national movements in Korea would sooner or later have adopted socialism or fascism.

Invention of the national identity, i.e., the imagined community, forges the recognition of the colonized and the passion toward the sublime object of one nation. It is in this way that the materiality of a nation-state comes to gain the symbolic dimension of existence. The symbolic ontology of a nation-state constructs the ideological core of nationalism: in a sense, the logic of form from within. In my view, this process of ideological symbolization is the essence of modernity.

Modernity as the human condition is another aspect of the nation-state. The self-consciousness of the colonized is to some extent an offshoot of modernity in that it relies on the feeling of a lost nation—one which never existed but which was allegedly always there in the past. The concept of self-determination endows it with the means to link concrete individuality to abstract nationality. As Thomas Hobbes described, the republic is the gigantic body of sovereignty, the integration of people and power. Once this imaginary corpus of a nation is fabricated, the dialectic of inclusion and exclusion begins. The inclusive and exclusive mechanisms give rise to discrimination regarding who is included in the nation and who is excluded, and the question of refugees emerges through the establishment of the nation-state. The presence of the refugee is the necessary by-product of modern nation-building based on the national right of self-determination.

In this sense, the refugee problem is not only a political issue but also constitutes the dark utopia of modernity that nationalism promises. There are many terms that indicate the risky aspects of human life in the condition of modernity, such as liquidity, precariousness, worldlessness, and so on. However, the essence of modern life is its homelessness. In this sense, the status of the refugee is not a particular mode of being but rather the general condition of human existence in the modern world. The homeostasis of a status "in between nation-states" could be called "refugee ontology." As has been discussed, there have since European Enlightenment thought been two indicators through which we can approach the existential question of the refugee: nationalism and cosmopolitanism. Interestingly, the status of the refugee was not seen as pitiful before the advent of the nation-state. For instance, Hugh de Saint-Victor, a medieval monk in the twelfth century, wrote the following:

> The person who finds his homeland sweet is a tender beginner; he to whom every soil is as his native one is already strong; but he is perfect to whom the entire world is as a foreign place. The tender soul has fixed his love on one spot in the world; the strong person has extended his love to all places; the perfect man has extinguished his.[5]

In his writing, Hugh de Saint-Victor claimed the state of exile and celebrated expatriate life. Interestingly, he described the deportee as "the strong person." He praised "foreign soil" because "it gives a man practice." Here, there is not the modern sense of the refugee as a commiserative creature but rather the archetypal cosmopolitan figure. For Hugh de Saint-Victor, "the strong person" or people are "those who philosophize," experiencing the world as "foreign soil."

The term *refugee* was invented in the seventeenth century and referred to Protestants who fled France following the recall in 1685 of the Edict of Nantes, which had granted them religious liberty and civil rights. Within a decade, the word came to describe those who are forced to flee to safety. The meaning of a refugee here gains exactly the opposite connotation of Hugh de Saint-Victor's strong person, the cosmopolitan image. As Immanuel Kant suggests, the ultimate goal of enlightened maturity for a civilized human being is to be cosmopolitan, not to limit him or herself to the national border. However, the status of the refugee in the modern sense shows a disturbing aspect of the Enlightenment project. The refugee, having been evicted, dispossessed, and excluded from the nation-state, exists in a transitional condition prior to its absorption by another state. A citizen *qua* refugee lives in the *inter*national space, i.e., the border between nation-states. The status of the refugee is not just temporary, instead showing us the substantial meaning of life today, life that is trapped by the national question.

This state of the refugee is not the problem of the Enlightenment as such. What is at stake here is the question of why the Kantian project, i.e., becoming cosmopolitan, fails, and why people quickly become refugees rather than *inter*national beings. As Hannah Arendt points out, "once they had left their homeland they remained homeless, once they had left their state they became stateless; once they had been deprived of their human rights they were rightless, the scum of the earth."[6] In discussion of the refugee, Arendt reveals that it is difficult to insist upon human rights in general if people do not belong to a specific national territory *within any borders*. Refugees are nothing less than homeless, stateless, rightless people who are ripped out of loci; in other words, they turn out to be "the scum of the earth" when they exit the borders of any nation-state.

Nationality is the precondition for human rights. A man's rights are not given automatically by natural law but are rather obtained through national citizenship. This is the paradox of human ontology in the modern age; we, human beings, have no self-evident right to reside in any place without nationality, even if we may travel across international borders. Rosa Luxemburg's insight on the national question returns here. There is no such thing as the absolute right of self-determination except in the nation-state as a historical phenomenon.

The real borders are nationality as such; those who fail to possess it are regarded as "the scum of the earth." Who or what is "the scum of the earth"? It means that refugees, those who do not have any national identification, are useless. Why useless? Because they have no legal right to work within any nation-state. Refugees are useless because they cannot be easily exchanged in the national relations of production. If a refugee wants to be exchanged in a specific nation-state, he or she must become a commodity.

Global capitalism, the new economic relationship among nation-states, means that only a commodity can freely cross national borders. This transnational situation seems to bring about the ideological basis for nationalism as well, i.e., the common sentiment that the nation-state can protect people from the global market. However, there is a discrepancy between the ideal of nationalism and the reality of the nation-state. Nationalism presupposes that all members of a nation are equal, while the nation-state as a bourgeois polity necessarily sustains the unequal relations of production. Even though the polity tends to transform into a technocratic one, promising the justice of competition, structural inequality in the capitalist mode of production cannot be solved because the means of production are always already taken by the political establishment.

The disparity between the nation-state and capitalism serves as the ideological perversion of nationalism. In Jacques Lacan's sense, perversion is not a form of behavior but a structure which disavows castration. From this perspective, nationalism is the perverse structure of ideology by which one perceives the lack of a nation (i.e., the primitive father) in a nation-state while refusing to accept the reality of this traumatic perception. Nationalism always already presumes the *Urgeschichte* (prehistory) of the nation and bolsters a fantasy that revolves around the loss of the authentic nation. No doubt, this national narrative would face trouble with the transnational and multicultural reality of global capitalism, but the conflict as such functions as an excuse to justify collective demands for national authenticity. Fascism is, in this sense, a political movement to forge social rebirth through the restoration of an authentic prehistoric nation in a radical way.

Unlike the tenets of fascist politics, liberalism strives to maintain the "justice" of the market and encourages the secularization or rationalization of the national imaginary. Nationalism should be allowed in the market as long as it recognizes the castration of the authentic nation. Here is where commodification functions as the binding mediation between nationalism and capitalism. Commodity fetishism transforms the ideal of nationalism into an earthly nation-state, i.e., the spatio-temporality of capitalism. The fetish effect based on commodity structures gives rise to an inversion by which exchange value becomes use value. If nationalism is to be exchangeable in the market, it must castrate its phallus—the nation. Ironically, this exchange value is the use value of nationalism in the nation-state. Nationalism without a nation—in other words, castrated nationalism—is nothing less than the condition of multiculturalism. In this sense, nation-states, the materiality of nationalism, serve as the markets of multiple nationalities in global capitalism.

Those with a nationality can exchange their labor power with monetary value. Once nationality is commodified, labor power as a commodity can be exchangeable in any nation-state. In this sense, the commodity is the opposite of the refugee. Its intermingling with the refugee problem is not about human rights but about capitalism's global division of labor. The presence of refugees forces us to rethink the political implications of the nation-state. The modern system of nationality is the by-product of nationalism's conformity to bourgeois economic interests. It is impossible to abolish it from without but necessary to reconstruct it from within because national consciousness, as Rosa Luxemburg clarifies, is used to mobilize the working classes in the competition to establish a strong nation-state. The paradox of Cold War ideology is revealed in this conformism. The anticommunism of the Cold War necessarily required international relations to help the nation-building of each country that had once been colonized, but it simultaneously resulted in national identity through international recognition. In this sense, it is not exceptional that the rise of the nation-state is observed after the end of the Cold War. The crisis of capitalism at the global level has also encouraged the prioritization of national interests over international collaboration. Now, we are about to witness the return of the national question following its emergence in the 1930s.

11.
Foucault and Iran

IN OCTOBER 1978, following his first visit to Iran, Michel Foucault met Ayatollah Khomeini, a symbolic figure of the Iranian revolution, at Khomeini's home in exile just outside Paris. Foucault made the decision to return to the country in November of the same year, when the revolutionary movement against the last shah of the Persian monarchy reached its peak. He was then commissioned as a correspondent by the Italian newspaper *Corriere della Sera*, and his original plan was to write about US President Jimmy Carter's international policy in the days of the Cold War, though he changed his mind during his first visit to the country. The Iranian Revolution engulfed his project. Before engaging with the Iranian situation, Foucault vehemently committed to the prisoners' rights movement via the *Groupe d'Information sur les Prisons*. Through his work with this group, Foucault became involved in the Iranian issue. Two French lawyers who helped Iranians in political exile brought the matter to Foucault's attention. He had already recognized Iran's political situation in 1977 when he joined Sartre and other French intellectuals in signing a letter in support of protests by the Writers' Association in Tehran. Foucault's interests in Iran were therefore not a digression from his work but an ongoing project of his political commitment.

His discovery of the Iranian revolution led him to the concept of "political spirituality" and his later works on ethics and the care of the self.[1] During the last few years of his life, Foucault suggested a link between spirituality and *parrhesia*—fearless speech. The revolutionary spirituality that he witnessed in Tehran led him to discover the possible exercise of transformative politics without European Enlightenment axioms. For Foucault, resistance on the street in Tehran demonstrated the self-creation of the ethical subject, creation through which people are willing to change themselves from the inside out. Through the spectacle of protest, Foucault grew curious about the reasons why people rose and the things they insisted. He described what the Iranians experienced as "the soul of the uprising."[2] He praised the Iranian protest for being a "true revolution" to bring out a "radical change in our experience," the transformation of "ourselves"—"our way of being, our relationship with others, with things, with eternity, with God."[3] How does this fundamental transition take place? More interestingly, Foucault suggested "the repetition of demonstration," i.e., the tireless demonstration of the people's will. He argued:

> Of course, it was not only because of the demonstrations that the shah left. But one cannot deny that it was because of an endlessly demonstrated rejection. There was in these demonstrations a link between collective action, religious ritual, and an expression of public right. It's rather like in Greek tragedy, where the collective ceremony and the reenactment of the principles of right go hand in hand. In the streets of Tehran there was an act, a political and juridical act, carried out collectively within religious rituals—an act of deposing the sovereign.[4]

What impressed Foucault was the "demonstrating" of the collective will, the command of general will in Rousseau's sense, which insisted on the principle of right against the sovereign and beyond. The French philosopher believed that he had encountered the collective will on the street in Tehran. He extended this experience into his view of history. Foucault did not merely describe the feeling of excitement but meticulously scrutinized the courage and the absence of fear that he saw in the scenes of protest. The formality of the repetition gave rise to political moments that cannot be reduced to the rational doctrine of the Enlightenment. Foucault's discovery of Iran could be regarded as a political engagement along the same lines as that of the postwar French intellectuals. This observation made his approach to the Iranian Revolution exceptional. He regarded the Islamic revolution not as an aberrant episode in a universal history but as a unique event without a commitment to rationalism. However, following the terrorist attacks of September 11, 2001, Foucault's affirmative evaluation of "political spirituality" was criticized as the erroneous consequence of a naive perspective on Islamism. For instance, Janet Afary and Kevin B. Anderson, the authors of *Foucault and the Iranian Revolution*, find the root of the horrific terrorism in the Iranian Revolution and its radical Islamic politics. They claim that the political extremism of Jihad is seduced by the "political spirituality" that Foucault valorized. Aside from Foucault, Afary and Anderson denounce Noam Chomsky and Howard Zinn for their defense of anti-imperialist Islamism, declaring that they "ignored the specific social and political context in which Al Qaeda arose, that of two decades of various forms of radical Islamist politics, beginning with the Iranian Revolution."[5] Against this argument, I will discuss the historical background of that concept and the influence of political Islamism on Foucault's turn in his later works. Foucault's understanding of the Iranian Revolution should be considered seriously in order to understand this theoretical shift.

Politics and Spirituality

Interestingly, Afary and Anderson consider the legacy of the Cold War to be one of the causes for these leftist or postmodernist attitudes toward Islamic politics. They argue that "most of the Left tended to view Islamism through the lens of Cold War politics, attributing its rise to 'blowback' from the US and Saudi Arabian-backed war against the Russians in Afghanistan."[6] Indeed, leftist analyses of Islamism and its relation to the Cold War are too reductive to explain why Foucault was fascinated with the Iranian Revolution and why, following his visit to Tehran, he turned his interest to Kant's question of the Enlightenment. Afary and Anderson do not properly deal with the political implications of the Iranian Revolution under the regime of the Cold War.

The Cold War began when the US took strategic responsibility for the world's economy, defining its shape in Europe and the Third World after World War II. The mission dovetailed with anticommunism, intending to drive the two regions to choose market economies. The US postwar task was to take over the periphery, which had sustained the international trading chain of the former imperial domains, such as Western Europe and Japan, and which had then moved toward becoming communist due to anti-imperialist resistance. Due to this rival vision of Americanism, Europe and the Third World lacked the necessity to increase their access to the US merchandising system. During this period, the Third World was mainly an ideological battlefield for capitalism and communism, and nationalism and Westernization. During this ideological competition, Western philosophy served as leverage to catalyze political movements in each national territory.

Against this geopolitical background, Foucault saw the Iranian Revolution as a third path between the USSR and the US, a possible politics beyond the frame of the Cold War. For this reason, Foucault's engagement with Iranian affairs and his theoretical shift to an affirmation of "political spirituality" must be regarded as an extension of his early philosophy, not the disillusionment of revolutionary fever. Behrooz Ghamari-Tabrizi correctly points out the meaning the Iranian Revolution had for Foucault's later works:

The Iranian Revolution was not the only political event to which Foucault paid close attention. For many years, he considered himself a part of a movement against penal injustice and for prisoners' rights, he supported the dissident Solidarity union movement in Poland and participated in activities in their defence, and he marched with protesters defending the rights of Vietnamese refugees. But no singular event in Foucault's history generated such a distinct transformation in his thought as the Iranian Revolution.[7]

By analyzing the Iranian Revolution to show how people could free themselves, Foucault defined structuralism not as a "document of impotence" but as a "philosophy or a manual of combat."[8] Referring to Lacan, Foucault emphasized the existence of the unconscious in defining the function of the subject. His reconsideration of structuralism is nothing less than a critique of modernization, which had already become archaic. In the first article he contributed to the Italian newspaper, Foucault described what had struck him at a bazaar in Tehran. There, he saw "unfit-for-use" sewing machines, which bore the inscription Made in South Korea. For Foucault, the products rendered visible the advent of Cold War economic globalization, rooted in the colonial legacy. The Western objects decorated with clumsy imitations of old Persian patterns symbolized the hollowness of modernity. Through this observation of the market scene, Foucault recognized the reality of modernization under Cold War capitalism, which was driven by the US in those days. Even the Carter administration in the US, the flag-bearer of human rights, supported Iranian despotism to compete with communism. The Cold War made it imperative for the US to compete with the USSR on its own terms by proving that a market economy could bring forth not just prosperity but justice, equality, and security. The political deadlock of the Cold War suppressed not only communism but all resistance from the bottom. The Cold War's ideological propaganda justified rampant state violence in the Third World. In this situation, political Islamism served as the third terrain by which the Iranian revolutionaries rejected both sides of the Cold War.

Regarding Foucault's concept of "political spirituality," what must be stressed is the combining of spirituality with politics. For Foucault, spirituality constitutes a desire to liberate the body from the prison of the soul. He regarded spirituality as having nothing to do with a religious doctrine, while he did not reject Shiite Islam as a source of "political spirituality." Therefore, it would be necessary to ask what kind of politics could be realized through spiritual practice. I contend that this question is about the rationale for Foucault's intervention in the Iranian Revolution. In his interview with Duccio Trombadori at the end of 1978, Foucault argued:

> What is history, given that there is continually being produced within it a separation of true and false? By that I mean four things. First, in what sense is the production and transformation of the true/false division characteristic and decisive for our historicity? Second, in what specific ways has this relation operated in Western societies, which produce scientific knowledge whose forms are perpetually changing and whose values are posited as universal? Third, what historical knowledge is possible of a history that itself produces the true/false distinction on which such knowledge depends? Fourth, isn't the most general of political problems the problem of truth? How can one analyze the connection between ways of distinguishing true and false and ways of governing oneself and others? The search for a new foundation for each of these practices, in itself and relative to the other, the will to discover a

different way of governing oneself through a different way of dividing up true and false—this is what I would call "political spirituality."⁹

Here, Foucault clarified that "political spirituality" is the will to found each of these practices, i.e., to distinguish true and false and govern oneself and others differently from the given establishment. The will to alter these practices is a transformative activity that must create a new beginning in order to change beyond its limits. For Foucault, truth is the regime of power for organizing the production, regulation, and distribution of discourse. Therefore, the regime of truth decides what is true and what is false. In this way, Foucault regards politics not as the scientific critique of ideological illusion but as the production of a new regime of truth. His concept of "political spirituality," i.e., the will to transform the given socioeconomic conditions, links the politics of truth to spirituality. Because of its theological implications, it would be easy to misunderstand this concept as a politics connected to religious faith. However, it is undeniable that Foucault's concept of "political spirituality" emphasizes the collective will to create the truth by transforming oneself. Above all, his idea of spirituality presupposes the desire for liberation.

Before travelling to Iran, Foucault intensively studied Ali Shari'ati's works, which hugely influenced the Iranian revolutionaries. I think this close reading of Shari'ati paved the way for Foucault's eventual turn toward the ethics of the self. For this reason, his affirmative approach to political Islamism was not the aberrant caprice of a naive French intellectual blinded by revolutionary fever. In *Marxism and Other Western Fallacies*, Shari'ati interpreted Islamic ideas by rigorously employing scientific concepts to provide the theoretical means for his audience. The purpose of Shari'ati's book was to defend Islam in an effort to bring together three dimensions of today's flows in religion, philosophy, and other human activity: mysticism, equality, and freedom. Alongside Shari'ati, Louis Massignon and his disciple, Henry Corbin, were another reference for Foucault's understanding of Islam. Even though Foucault came across Shari'ati and Corbin, he did not know that the hidden sources for Iranian revolutionary thought came from Western philosophy. One of them was Martin Heidegger.

Against "Westoxification"

For Shari'ati, modernization is the sickness that follows the disease of "Westoxification." Heidegger's philosophy, he argued, could save Islamic people from this illness by teaching them the real face and spirit of the West. Above all, Heidegger's concept of authenticity was regarded as the theoretical basis upon which Iranian readers, already influenced by Sartre's existentialism, could envision an alternative to Westernization. In the Iranian context, Heidegger's notion of authenticity, *Eigentlichkeit*, is used normatively to denote an ontological distinction between the owned life and the disowned life, even though Heidegger himself occasionally employs it for a description of *Dasein*'s unowned life between the authentic and the inauthentic. Shari'ati's critique of Westernization echoed Ahmad Fardid, a professor of philosophy at the University of Tehran. Fardid was the established authority who was primarily responsible for bringing such an interpretation of Heidegger to Iran. Fardid studied Western philosophy at Sorbonne University and the University of Heidelberg. After his return to Iran, he organized the Iranian Heideggerian research group in the 1970s. Unlike the prolific Shari'ati, who brought together Marxism and Third Worldism in his writings, Fardid's philosophical framework stayed faithful to Heidegger's original critique of a decadent West.

However, Fardid's Iranian Heideggerian group functioned as a meeting place where Iranian intellectuals exchanged opinions about many political issues. They appropriated Heidegger's philosophy to serve their ideas of the modern world from a non-European perspective, i.e., through political Islamism. For them, Heidegger's Greeks, representing the ideal life against the decline of their time, were analogous with the Orient, i.e., the spiritual life of Islam. For both Heidegger and Fardid, the authentic mode of existence provided a radical basis for reevaluating one's being. From this perspective, Fardid's Iran would be the chosen nation in between capitalism and communism, like Heidegger's Germany. Fardid regarded Westernization as a passage toward Islamic self-realization, and Heidegger would be a motivator for the revival of Islamism. Shari'ati advanced Fardid's interpretations of Heidegger by revitalizing Shiism. His concepts of Red Shiism and Black Shiism attempted to split Islamism into two halves. Red Shiism is the pure form of religion concerning social justice and salvation, while Black Shiism is the deviated form of religion dominated by monarchy and clergy. The former exists for people's liberation, but the latter is sustained in the service of powerful elites out of touch with people's needs. Shari'ati's notion of Red Shiism is the theoretical basis on which Foucault elaborates his concept of "political spirituality."

Due to the invocation of the color red, Shari'ati's theory of political Islamism was identified with communism during the Cold War era, and most of the traditional Islamic leaders, except Ayatollah Khomeini, did not support Shari'ati's position. What should be stressed here is that Shari'ati's Red Shiism, despite his definition of it as a pure religious form, is nothing less than a religious practice for social justice and salvation. Some critics attempt to find an affinity between political Islamism and Heidegger's critique of liberal democracy and tend to conclude that Heidegger's philosophy has an inner logic employed by the anti-Western Islamists. However, I would like to argue that Heidegger's relation to the West was ambivalent because his philosophical vision could not find its political solution in any *realpolitik,* even when he supported Hitler. His critique gained its justification through the reality of Western imperialism, but his political faith in the National Socialist Party failed to escape the impasse of the nation-state. His philosophy was pursued desperately to retrieve the forgotten Hellenic origins of the West amid a fallen world of nihilism and technological madness. In this way, his concept of authenticity, far from being a political failure, enabled the Iranian intellectuals to reject the inauthentic historicity of the monarchy.

Islamic Heideggerianism

It might be easy to argue that there are theoretical affinities between Heidegger's philosophy and Iranian Islamism in their anti-Western tendency and their rejection of liberal democracy. However, the Iranian reception of Heidegger was not the consequence of Islamic fundamentalism. The Iranians' refusal of modernization did not mean that they wanted to retreat from the secular world to the heavenly sanctuary of God; suffering from the anticommunist and anti-Islamic monarchy, they wanted to build an Islamic utopia in their country. Ironically, Fardid, Shari'ati and other anti-Western Iranian intellectuals—e.g., Jalal Al-e Ahmad, Darius Shayegan, Reza Davari, and Abdolkarim Soroush—knew Western philosophy very well and were open to the ideas of Western intellectuals. Even Ayatollah Khomeini, the religious leader of the Iranian Revolution, backed these Westernized anti-Western intellectuals. Ayatollah Khomeini's meeting with Foucault and his support for political Islamism indicate that their anti-Western Islamism was not a reactionary politics against the West itself. Above all, the credit for such a radical anti-Western tendency revolving around the Iranian Revolution must be attributed to the actual experience of living under the Western-backed monarchy of the shah. The Iranian state of exception was violently forced into existence through a military coup in 1953. A decade later, the Western imposition of democratic experimentation began with the Iranian people's aspiration toward republicanism. The fomentation of anti-Western tendencies originated with Iranian mistrust of the West, and as a result, Heidegger's critique of an inauthentic West was ready to be adopted by an Iranian political movement that sought to retrieve a lost authenticity.

Shari'ati's political vision, which influenced Foucault's insight into "political spirituality," intends to bring together people, ideology, and God into a unified force. He believes that this unified wholeness will rescue people from the trap of irresponsible and clueless liberalism. God is not the symbolic object of religious worship here but the political authority for organizing a mass movement. Shari'ati's background consists of a God-worshipping socialist group in which his father was involved and his education in Paris from the late 1950s to the early 1960s. While residing in Paris—which was not a typical European city, and which was at that time the world's hub for cultural and political movements—Shari'ati witnessed both intellectual resistance against the French government's colonial rule in Algeria and a scene of unrestrained philosophical debate among Camus, Sartre, Aron, de Beauvoir, Merleau-Ponty, Lefort, etc. He knew well that not all of the West is necessarily bad. Therefore, it would be unfair to declare that his appeal to Islamic utopianism is simply the voice of fundamentalism. Shari'ati argued:

> We are clearly standing on the frontier between two eras, one where both Western civilization and Communist ideology have failed to liberate humanity, drawing it instead into disaster and causing the new spirit to recoil in disillusionment; and where humanity in search of deliverance will try a new road and take a new direction, and will liberate its essential nature. Over this

dark and dispirited world, it will set a holy lamp like a new sun; by its light, the man alienated from himself will perceive anew his primordial nature, rediscover himself, and clearly see the path of salvation. Islam will play a major role in this new life and movement.[10]

I think what Shari'ati is saying here reveals that his vision is to bring forth politics alternative to the West-imposed straitjacket of the Cold War and in response to the failure of the Enlightenment. Shari'ati's critique of Marxism and existentialism is strategic and even persuasive when he defines dialectical materialism as "material monotheism."[11] For him, the Iranian situation was a consequence of the failed utopian project, alienating humanity from its primal nature. Salvation is, in this sense, another term to indicate the liberation of the essential human nature from any tyranny. However, liberation is only possible if one affirms God, an absolute category for embracing the primordial stance of all multiple objects beyond representation. Shari'ati's political Islamism explains why the Iranian Revolution attracted Foucault. What is most important is that the Iranian revolutionaries used Heidegger to reformulate traditional Islam for their political Islamism. As Gilles Deleuze once said, a theory is a box of tools that must be useful and functional in its experimental exercise.[12] Heidegger in Tehran is an example to prove what Deleuze conceptualizes as the use of a theory.

God and Disjunction

After the banishment to Lucena of Ibn Rushd, who is more familiar to Europe by his Latin name Averroës, philosophy was regarded as heresy in the Islamic world. The philosophical debate between al-Ghazali and Ibn Rushd ended when the latter was ejected and his works were destroyed. Ibn Rushd tried to prove the usefulness of philosophy for promoting religious belief and insisted that philosophy is the most sophisticated form of religion. Against this idea, al-Ghazali questioned the apparent contradiction between reason and revelation and sought another solution for the reconciling of philosophy and religion. The use of Heidegger by Iranian intellectuals in the 1970s should be seen against this Islamic philosophical background. The intellectuals recognized the schism between philosophy and religion, yet they employed Heidegger's critique of the West to politicize Islam. In my opinion, the rise of political Islamism can be ascribed to Cold War geopolitics. On the surface, the postwar US mission pretended to support human rights and liberty, but underneath the civilized facade, its policies secretly aided the premodern tyranny of the shah and connived in the worst form of state-directed violence against civilians. The geopolitical hypocrisy collided with the Iranians' passion for their republic and grounded the circumstances in which the Iranians rejected both the US and the USSR for a path in between. For them, abolishing the anti-Islamic monarchy was an urgent task that would bring forth the authentic republic.

The Iranian revolutionaries weaponized philosophy to radicalize their religious faith and to pursue a middle path during the Cold War. The Iranian case shows that the function of philosophy is to create an intermediate zone beyond the boundary of any territory. I think that the Iranian Revolution is one of many cases showing the realization of such philosophical universalism. What Foucault encountered in Tehran would be the incarnation of the truth. The Iranian *realpolitik*, the realization of political theocracy as an alternative to liberalism, is likely what attracted Foucault. In his earlier lectures at the Collège de France from 1972 to 1973, Foucault teased out problems buried deep in the Hobbesian presupposition of sovereignty. Unlike in Hobbes's conclusion, the birth of a sovereign disciplinary power does not end the war between individuals but instead brings forth a war within the state, i.e., a civil war. The establishment of sovereign violence is not the suspension of *bellum omnium contra omnes* but the return of the repressed war of all against all.

Foucault pointed out that the principle of quasi equality carries with it a state of constant war, preserving the dimension of distrust. According to him,

> The individual as such, in his relationship with others, is the bearer of this permanent possibility of the war of all against all. If there is in fact a war of all against all, it is first of all essentially because men are equal in the objects and ends they set their sights on, because they are equivalent in the means they possess for obtaining what they seek. They are, as it were, substitutable for each other, and that is precisely why they seek to replace each other and, when something is offered to the desire of one, the other may always substitute himself for the first, wanting to take his place and appropriate what he desires. This substitutability, this convergence of desire characterizes this original competition.[13]

Each individual cannot resist the fact that anyone could take their place. This never-ending competition among nation-state members is the most critical feature that constitutes the enactment of sovereign power. For this reason, there might be no constitutional foundation for the nation-state without the dominant ruler. In Foucault's sense, the political solution to the civil war is to invent a glorious person who prevails over others with additional power. This balance of power based on the person with additional power must be rendered workable; otherwise, outright civil war will erupt, and the nation-state will fall into crisis. A bearer of sovereign authority is therefore necessary for modern liberal constitutions. Foucault's concept of "political spirituality" results from his observation of Iran's attempt to overcome this problem of liberal democracy, and this concept fundamentally rejects an antidemocratic solution.

As is well known, Carl Schmitt also indicated the supreme power's essential role in the modern state. He criticized liberal democracy as a political deception because it operates as if there is no exceptional decision-maker. For Schmitt, the legal order cannot function without a sovereign authority's decisions. He argued that "whether God alone is sovereign, that is, the one who acts as his acknowledged representative on earth, or the emperor, or prince, or the people, the question is always aimed at the subject of sovereignty."[14] From this perspective, Schmitt concluded that dictatorship is the only solution to the "metaphysical kernel of all politics."[15] Interestingly, Schmitt criticized Hobbes's political philosophy for being the consequence of mathematical relativism. According to Schmitt, Hobbes's critical mistake is that he did not justify dictatorship in the absence of legitimacy, even though the founder of political philosopher also recognized the pivotal role of "decisionist thinking." In Schmitt's sense, the sovereign is none other than the one who decides on the state of exception. Even in a theocracy, there must be a human being, a particular personality, who chooses to renew the legitimacy. Religion is, thus, one of many political forms, not an apolitical realm.

Schmitt's political theory clarifies to some extent the weakest link in modern representative democracy; however, it simultaneously gives rise to the dilemma of dictatorship. Schmitt defended the decisionism of dictatorship, anticipating the Last Judgment against atheist-anarchist politics. Schmitt deplored that "American financiers, industrial technicians, Marxist socialists, and anarchic-syndicalist revolutionaries unite in demanding that the biased rule of politics over unbiased economic management be done away with."[16] For him, the separation of politics from the economy is the essence of representative politics. Due to this depoliticizing logic in modern democracy, "there must no longer be political problems, only organizational-technical and economic-sociological tasks."[17] Shari'ati also apprehended this fundamental problem within liberal democracy, and his political Islamism aimed at reviving politics against its apolitical economism. However, Shari'ati did not accept Schmitt's solution. Unlike Schmitt's approval of dictatorship as a theological variation, Shari'ati emphasized the paradoxical relationship between God and humans—"A simultaneous denial and affirmation, a becoming nothing and all, essentially an effacement and a transformation into a divine being during natural, material life."[18] In other words, God serves as a supplement to humanity, and its existence founds the disjunctive synthesis of life. Life should not be reduced to the binary logic of contradiction and must affirm the paradox of its multiplicity. God functions as an immanent drive, continuously liberating humanity from its corporeal limit.

Foucault's position is much closer to Shari'ati's than to Schmitt's. In an interview in 1977, Foucault pointed out that "we are perhaps living the end of politics," and then added that "politics is a field which was opened by the existence of the revolution, and if the question of revolution can no longer be asked in these terms, then politics risks disappearing."[19] No doubt, the Iranian Revolution enabled him to confirm what he said—the rebirth of politics through revolution.

Unlike the claims of mischievous Western propaganda, the establishment of Islamic theocracy was a realistic solution to the limits of liberal democracy. The disjunctive dualism of political Islamism, affirming the difference between representative democracy and God's decision on exception, suggests an alternative to Schmitt's solution concerning liberal democracy. God's state of emergency will return when the constitutional institution stops working. In this way, God is nothing other than the void of sovereign power, prohibiting any human tyrant who would occupy the locus of supremacy. Only divine violence can possess the authority to suspend the legal system and declare a state of exception. God is not the single bearer of sovereignty but rather the revelation of unrepresentative politics, which provides the basis for liberation from the representative power. Foucault's concept of "political spirituality" should be grasped along with the idea that political Islamism solves a problem innate to the political system of liberalism. Foucault clearly stated that the Iranian movement was strong enough to abolish the dictatorship "when people attempted to inscribe the figures of spirituality on political ground."[20] This courageous decision to transform the regime of truth was made by the collective will, attempting to create another departure from political practice. Therefore, "political spirituality" has nothing to do with political theology, instead abolishing the theological legacy in politics. The spirituality of the Iranians who fought to their deaths affirmed not individual salvation but the establishment of an Islamic republic. This revolutionary goal is quite different from Schmitt's when he identified a person who decides on exceptions with theological authority. Not surprisingly, Foucault defines "the arts of existence," i.e., the care of the self, as "those intentional and voluntary actions by which men not only set themselves rules of conduct, but also seek to transform themselves, to change themselves in their singular being, and to make their life into an oeuvre."[21] In this sense, it is not difficult to say that his ethical project originated in "political spirituality," seeking the infinite liberation of the self from a given regime of truth rather than self-management in the name of individual interests.

12.

North Korea and the Enigma of Survival

DESPITE THE FOCUS OF THE ORIENTALIST MEDIA, North Korea is not an enigma. The mere fact of its "brute existence" shouldn't seduce or astonish us any more than the "diversity" of the capitalist system that seemingly hems it in on all sides. And yet its stubborn survival, much like that of capitalism, *is* quite arguably an enigma. The question of North Korea today is that of the political endurance and continuity of a regime whose "social experiment" should long ago have been jettisoned into the dustbin of history. Its blanket demonization and ostracism by the "international community" is proof of a profoundly abnormal country, a zombie state which certainly resists the norms of the modern liberal state. As Jon Halliday once put it, "no state in the world lives with such a wide gap between its own self-image and self-presentation as a socialist 'paradise on earth' and the view of most of the rest of the world that it is a bleak, backward workhouse ruled by a megalomaniac tyrant, Kim Il Sung."[1] Yet, all appearances aside, what I want to suggest is that there is a rational kernel at work here, not so much "beneath" the thin veneer of paranoid propaganda that comprises its overtly repressive state apparatus but in terms of North Korea's position within the uneven and combined development of global capitalism. All appearances aside, North Korea has been strongly committed to the process of modernization since its foundation, even if in this respect the ideology is invariably prone to part company with the reality, as the much-trumpeted "successes" of its social plan become ever more symptomatic of massive and grotesque system failure.

North Korea didn't fall suddenly from the sky. The evil features of this "hermit kingdom" have grown out of the traits of the modern state itself. Journalistic platitudes and general bias aside, North Korea is not a feudal state or an anachronistic theocracy but a nation-state with both an obsessive attitude toward modernization and a strong ambition to be one of the world's most advanced countries. Superman didn't land in North Korea. However, in *Superman: Red Son*,[2] Mark Millar presents us with a counterfactual history that explores what might have happened if the rocket ship carrying the young alien from Krypton had landed on Earth slightly earlier. In this scenario, the "advanced" landing deposits the future superhero in Ukraine, where instead of growing up in the free state of Kansas and becoming a journalist at the *Daily Planet*, he grows up on a collective farm and becomes a journalist at *Pravda*. One needs to set aside one's prejudices in order to begin to bring North Korea into proper focus—although such formal reversals of good versus evil are limited in their critical scope. The "monstrosity" of North Korea is nothing less than the unmasked identity of the modern state, the naked face of state violence. What one should question here is not what kind of country North Korea is but instead what North Korea contributes to the question of modernity and to modernization more specifically. In short, the supposedly "enigmatic" aspect of North Korea lies in the extremity of its modernization, which is a process that was pursued by both the socialist bloc and the capitalist bloc in the postwar world. The North Korean question should therefore be revised in order to ask why the process of modernization along with democratization results in the strange accomplishment of the country's secular theocratic regime.

The Democratic Paradox

The political ambitions of North Korea as a modern state seem to lurk in its official name: The Democratic People's Republic of Korea (DPRK). Like South Korea, North Korea insists on being the only legitimate government of the entire peninsula. What must be stressed here is that North Korea calls itself a democratic people's republic, unlike South Korea, which is a simple republic (ROK), whose people are absent twice, so to speak: neither a people nor a *demos*. However, the term "democratic people's republic" might be a tautology or double negation, as *democracy* indicates a government of the people and *republic* is derived from *res publica*, i.e., public affairs or commonwealth. The terminological repetition perhaps betrays North Korea's obsession with modernization and nation-building under the direction of the country's communist party, the Workers' Party of Korea.

Kim Il Sung, who was the country's visionary leader—not to mention its deity—was the Superman sent down from Soviet heaven to construct a new country. According to North Korea's propaganda, Kim promised his people daily rations of "rice and meat soup" for participating in guerrilla warfare against the Japanese imperialists. After liberation, the guerilla figure took power during the Soviet occupation and began to implement a strongly partisan agenda. As in other postcolonial countries, Kim Il Sung and his followers first set about reinventing the past. The situation whereby the North Korean leader created the racial self-image of his nation is described in the following terms:

> Though most Koreans in 1945 had no memory of life before Japanese rule, neither the Soviets nor the Americans saw a need to de-colonize hearts and minds. That the Koreans now hated Japan was taken as proof that they had always done so. Nor did either power punish

former propagandists. In Seoul, the cultural scene's spontaneous efforts to come to terms with its past were soon undermined by the settling of personal scores and a general refusal to acknowledge a collective guilt. Obscure ex-collaborators condemned the famous ones, those who had propagandized in Korean asserted moral superiority over those who had done so in Japanese, and erstwhile "proletarians" acted as if their brief prison stays in the 1930s made up for everything they had written afterward.[3]

When Korea was liberated from colonialism, a blank-slate scenario emerged in which anybody who obtained power could fabricate anything about history. This situation provided the perfect conditions for modernization. Even though Kim Il Sung was once a commander in Mao Zedong's army and spent a year at an infantry officer school in the USSR during the Pacific War, his ideological background was unlikely to have familiarized him a great deal with Marxism-Leninism. As North Korean propaganda frequently emphasizes today, he was in those days more inclined to an alliance between socialism and nationalism. He even insisted that Korea had reached the stage of democratic reform and construction, not socialism as such.[4] Needless to say, this does not mean that North Korea came to "communism" via nationalism. The communist regime was implanted in Korea by the USSR and backed up by the Red Army from the time of its foundation.[5] Challenging the nationalist intellectuals such as Cho Man Sik, Kim attempted to consolidate his support base and mobilized more people to participate in constructing his regime.

The official name of North Korea indicates the historical background of Kim's nation-building project. The "democratic people" are those who join in the process of democratic reform and construction against the US-led world order. The tautological emphasis on the people who advocate democracy, i.e., the rule of the common people, reveals the "democratic paradox" as such: if everybody rules, who would be ruled? As Carl Schmitt points out, those who command and those who obey are identical in democracy.[6] If democracy means that the sovereign of an assembly composed of all people can change the laws and constitution at will, the question of who belongs to the people and who does not remains. In this respect, it must be determined who belongs to the people that can decide the law at will. Accordingly, the "Democratic People's Republic" is simultaneously inclusive and exclusive in its constitutional arrangements. As the very basis of its constitution, it seeks to include those who agree on democratic reform and construction and exclude those who disagree.

Chantal Mouffe regards Schmitt's definition of democracy as the means by which a people comes to exist through the determination of who should be included and who should be excluded. She says, "Without any criterion to determine who are the bearers of democratic rights, the will of the people could never take shape."[7] Of course, this definition of "democracy" is arguably at odds with liberal accounts of democracy. However, Schmitt's critique of liberal democracy is in some sense amenable to the constitutional dynamics of North Korea. Clearly, North Korea endorses not liberal democracy but the dictatorship of the proletariat. Interestingly, there is a crucial clue to Kim Il Sung's *political* concept of democracy in his 1967 speech on the dictatorship of the proletariat. In these remarks, Kim criticized both "the Right opportunist view" and "the Left opportunist view" on the dictatorship of the proletariat in relation to the transition period following the communist revolution. He then set out his own theory of a third way, the so-called *Juche*. To quote from the speech:

> We must take into account such specific realities of ours in order to give correct solutions to the questions of the

transition period and the dictatorship of the proletariat. Bearing this point in mind, I consider it excessive to regard the transition period in our country as the period up to the higher phase of communism. I deem it right to regard it as the period up to socialism. But it is wrong to believe that the transition period will come to a close as soon as the socialist revolution is victorious and the socialist system is established. Considering the issue on the basis of what the founders of Marxism-Leninism said, or considering it in the light of the experiences we have gained in our actual struggle, we cannot say that a complete socialist society is already built just because the capitalist class has been overthrown and the socialist revolution carried through after the seizure of power by the working class. We, therefore, have never said that the establishment of the socialist system means the complete victory of socialism. Then, when will the complete socialist society come into being? Complete victory of socialism will come only when the class distinction between the workers and the peasantry has disappeared and the middle classes (particularly the peasant masses) actively support us.[8]

According to Kim's argument, the problem is not so much the transformation of the capitalist mode of production into a socialist one as that of the *"working-classization"* of the middle classes. Kim points out that "as long as the peasants are not *working-classized*, the support they may give us cannot be firm and is bound to be rather unstable."[9] How then is social transformation to be achieved? Kim places the emphasis on rapid economic development as the means for the consolidation of socialism. He argues that "to this end, the technological revolution should be carried out to such an extent as the advanced capitalist countries have turned their countryside capitalistic, so that farming may be mechanized, chemicalization and irrigation be introduced, and the eight-hour day be adapted."[10]

This utterance reveals the meaning of *working-classizing* the peasants. Despite railing against the orthodox doctrine of Marxism-Leninism, forever emphasizing how North Korean realities differ from those of Europe and Russia, Kim's theory of socialism is a somewhat truncated and circular argument that outlines how the stable material basis for socialism is to be achieved: socialism is its own theory's goal. This is nothing new for anyone familiar with Stalin's theory of socialism in one country. In his letter to Ivan Philipovich Ivanov, "On the Final Victory of Socialism in the USSR," Stalin claimed that socialism in one country does not mean the final accomplishment of revolution and that the international alliance of the proletariat can solve the problem of one-state socialism, adding that "this assistance of the international proletariat must be combined with our work to strengthen the defense of our country, to strengthen the Red Army and the Red Navy, to mobilize the whole country for the purpose of resisting military attack and attempts to restore bourgeois relations."[11]

What should be stressed in Kim's speech is not his vulgar reception of Stalinism but rather his reformulation of Stalinist ideas. Kim rejects Stalin's assumption that the USSR has successfully purged the legacy of bourgeois society and asks, somewhat rhetorically, "What, then, shall we say is the society that will exist after the triumph of the socialist revolution and accomplishment of socialist transformation, until the disappearance of the class distinction between the workers and the peasants?"[12] Kim even insists that the dictatorship of the proletariat must continue in order to eliminate class differences. This point is crucial for understanding the ideological structure of nation-building in North Korea. As Barbara Demick observes, Kim did not merely seek "to build a new country; he wanted to build better people, to reshape human nature."¹³ This project to reconstruct consciousness is called *Juche*, which means the independence of the people. Its doctrine is one of "holding fast to an independent position, rejecting dependence on others, using one's own brains, believing in one's own strength, displaying the revolutionary spirit of self-reliance."¹⁴ It certainly sounds like the liberal rubric of self-government. Nevertheless, one distinctive aspect can be identified in the ideology of *Juche*: the confidence of the people in their leader is essential for the establishment of such independence. This is where the psychic life of power is introduced into the political.

The Monstrosity of North Korea

North Korea may indeed be characterized as grotesque, but it is not the "Impossible State." Victor Cha describes North Korea as being caught between life and death after the collapse of the "mighty Soviet Union."¹⁵ Cha's understanding of North Korea betrays the typical bias shown toward the country, where North Korea is often misrecognized thanks to the liberal prism of democracy. It is intriguing that Cha does not seem to properly grasp the meaning of North Korea, and that he confesses his inability to solve the enigma of its survival. He suggests that the reason North Korea has survived—though "many others of its ilk have long since collapsed, and as revolutions in the Middle East and North Africa spell the demise of the few remaining ones like it"—resides in the over-the-top personality cult of the Kim family.¹⁶ Cha correctly brings into focus what Kim Il Sung intended with the term *Juche*. The doctrine of *Juche* is nothing less than the secular version of Christianity, wherein fidelity to the figure of authority sets one free from the fear of the death. What Kim achieved was to replace God with the "dear respected leader comrade." However, this alleged idolization of a singular political leader applies not only to

North Korea. The problem of this singular sovereign is not just the problem of North Korea but that of the modern state in general.

In *North Korea: Beyond Charismatic Politics*, Heonik Kwon and Byung-Ho Chung discuss the general aspects of North Korea as a modern state by invoking Max Weber's concept of charismatic politics. Kwon and Chung argue that:

> There is actually no mystery about the North Korean political system. The North Korean state is not an enigmatic entity and never has been. North Korea had a highly skillful political leader who knew how to build an aura of captivating charismatic power. This leader understood the efficacy of this power for mobilizing the masses toward ambitious political goals, and he was committed to keeping that power not only during his lifetime but also beyond the time of his rule. Modern world history abounds with similar charismatic, visionary leaders and the stories of their rises and falls. The same is true in the political history of the communist world that constituted the moiety of the Cold War international order.[17]

Kwon and Chung resist the demonization of the communist regime and instead attempt to deconstruct the fetishism of liberal democracy. They point out that "the performance of secular revolutionary politics, while aiming to demystify traditional religious norms and mystical ideas … often involved the mystification of the authority and power of the revolutionary leadership."[18] As they rightly claim, what is at issue is not the cult of personality but its sustainability in North Korea. How does North Korea's charismatic politics outlive others? According to Weber, any charismatic authority must be subject to "interpretation or development in an anti-authoritarian direction."[19] He conceptualizes this principle of the antiauthoritarian direction as the "transformation of charisma." If the enchanted charisma of the political leader is supposed to lose its enchantment through the process of modernization, the case of North Korea would seem to suggest that Weber's theory of charismatic politics is problematic.

For Weber, the concept of charisma is related to religious dogmatism. In this sense, he confirms the way in which the progress of rationalization in "the organization of the corporate group" demystifies the charismatic authority for whom universal respect was once a duty. From this perspective, it is easy to conclude that the ruling ideology of *Juche* contaminates North Koreans and impedes them from progressive rationalization. However, as Weber admits, the charismatic leader cannot sustain himself without the people's free will: "The leader whose legitimacy rested on his personal charisma" should be followed by the political support of those who are "formally free to elect and elevate to power as they please and even to depose."[20] Through free elections, the leader loses his or her charisma and, in turn, their genuine legitimacy. And yet it seems that Kim Il Sung and his partisan comrades successfully and "freely" manage to champion and sustain their legitimacy whilst retaining a charisma that goes hand in hand with modernization. This is where the central question arises. If North Korea thrives on defending its charismatic politics, is it really valid to regard it, formally speaking, as a model socialist country? This question currently animates the political group of left nationalists in South Korea, who still concur on the pan-national authenticity of North Korea.

It seems that the problem with Weber's theory lies in his identification of rationalization or modernization with the marketization of capitalism. His conceptualization of charisma is descriptive and does not fit the situation of North Korea. In light of this weakness, Kwon and Chung put forward the concept of a "theater state" to account for the endurance of North Korean politics, citing the works of Clifford Geertz, Wada Haruki and Carol Medlicott.[21] In short, North Korea is a theater state in which all members of the community play a part while simultaneously watching "the drama of power transfer from the country's founding leader, Kim Il Sung, to his eldest son and the country's former leader, Kim Jong Il."[22] With this concept, Wada also underscores North Korea's obsession with the transmission of power through generations and regards it as the ritualization of its partisan tradition. Wada's adoption of the theater state concept seems clear; he seems to attribute the grotesque dimensions of North Korea to its premodern or feudal remnants. Furthermore, Medlicott argues that "the North Korean political order is fundamentally Confucian."[23] However, outright displays of affection toward the beloved leader hardly provide crucial evidence that North Koreans are immersed in Confucianism. As Bryan Myers points out, "almost all cultures espouse respect for one's parents, and kinship metaphors have been part of political language since time immemorial."[24] In this sense, it seems that Wada's and Medlicott's premise, commonly shared by other North Korea commentators such as Kwon and Chung, neglects the bigger picture. Their concept of a "theater state" is too anthropological, too mired in the myths of "primitive peoples," to capture the uniqueness of North Korea and its political regime.

The theatrical spectacle of power is just a symptom and not the cause of the grotesque. The theory of a "theater state" reiterates the problem that Weber's theory of charismatic politics reveals when applied to North Korea as a unique case of the modern state. These approaches fail to gain access to the truth of North Korea. The spectacle they validate as evidence of premodern ritualization has nothing to do with the regressive re-enchantment of the secular theocracy. My contention is that the theocratic aspect of North Korea is the hidden truth of the modern state as such, the brutal revelation of extreme modernization. Its grotesque spectacle is to be discerned as the mirror image of Western modernity.

The North Korean Lesson

In *Secret State: Inside North Korea*, Will Ripley's CNN special report of 2017, a North Korean boy whose birthday party is being prepared by his school informs the foreign journalist that the dear respected leader, Kim Jung Un, cares for him and his classmates more than their own parents do, and gives them more love than their parents could ever provide. Setting aside the ideological agenda of such hot media, the journalist seems to take the interview with the boy as confirmation of an ultrapaternalistic leadership in North Korea. Should we be surprised by the deep roots of such authoritarian constitutions, of which North Korea is admittedly an extreme variety? Cicero wrote, "Since our country provides more benefits and is a parent prior to our biological parents, we have a greater obligation to it than to our parents."[25] The idea of a parental constitution, or the fundamental bond that links *pater familias* and *res publica*, does in actual fact pose an intriguing philosophical question. As Jochen Martin has argued, according to Ann-Cathrin Harders,

> those aspects concerning the agnatic *familia* and the power of the *paterfamilias* are not to be taken as "private" aspects relegated to domestic life. Instead they are essential to the political and social organization of the *res publica Romana*—especially the extensive powers of the *paterfamilias*, his *ius vitae necisque*, have to be paralleled to the magistrates' *potestas*.[26]

One should be wary of trying to transpose a fully-fledged politics from the domestic realm into the realm of real politics and the executive power of the state, which in the case of North Korea amounts to the charismatic leadership of a sole figure. In the Roman context, the authority of the *pater familias* was limited—"embedded"—by and within the overriding terms of the *res publica*. Occasions were few when the *pater familias* could act on behalf of the state and take the law into his own hands.[27] One should be equally wary of practicing Orientalism by contriving to make North Korea conform to certain "universal" patterns of political constitution, whose foundation of the parental constitution is also derived from the Roman idea of authority.[28] For those who consume North Korea as a spectacle of grotesque political failure, its outlandish society cannot fail to be mysterious or, better still, exotic. Nonetheless, the "strangeness" of North Korea is intelligible through the experience of foreign intervention and its encounter with Western political traditions. As Myers argues, North Korea's conflation of nationalism with socialism was founded on the "blood-based Japanese nationalism of the colonial era."[29] Like South Korea, the whole nation-building process in North Korea is "the slavish imitation of foreign models and an often contemptuous indifference to indigenous traditions."[30]

Kim Il Sung himself emphasized a break from the traditions of feudalism and urged his people to remodel everyday life according to the USSR's superior culture. Kim's compulsion to modernize North Korea was consistent with his theory of a socialism conceived in terms of *Juche*. Adopting Lenin's New Economic Policy, Kim set up the Seven-Year Plan to remove the residues of feudalism:

> The fundamental tasks of the Seven-Year Plan are to carry out the all-round technical and cultural revolution on the basis of the triumphant socialist system, thereby laying the solid material and technical foundations of socialism and greatly improving the material and cultural life of the people.
>
> In a country like ours, where there were no industrial revolution and normal stages of capitalist

development in the past, the technical revolution poses itself as a task of special importance during the socialist construction. In conformity with the urgent demands of social development, we have completed the socialist transformation of production relations before the technical reconstruction of the national economy, thereby opening up a broad avenue for the development of the productive forces, particularly for the carrying out of the technical revolution.[31]

It is not difficult to detect in this speech Kim's foregrounding of the "technical revolution." Needless to say, this is a complete perversion of Marx's insistence on the driving *contradiction* between the forces and relations of production. Interestingly, Kim identifies the technical revolution with the cultural revolution. In a characteristically circular argument, the construction of the *modern* nation-state is the *raison d'État* of North Korea as a socialist state. For Kim, the accomplishment of self-reliance and self-defense is the only way toward the correct form of socialism. Kim's grandson, Kim Jung Un, is taking this enthusiasm to its logical extreme through the development of nuclear missile technology.

It is undeniable that Kim's regime has resisted the secularization of charisma and has succeeded in defending its authority while ruthlessly pursuing the country's modernization. These two features of the regime strongly condition each other. Nevertheless, we must still return to the question of how the charismatic leadership has managed to remain intact. Although it is often called a pseudotheocracy, the political regime of the North is strongly animated by the idea of the modern nation-state. Countless observers regard North Korea as a premodern state ruled by sovereign power, but the North Korean incarnation of the state form inevitably shares the disciplinary imperative characteristic of demands to manage people and the real or imaginary threat of enemy populations. As Michel Foucault argues, disciplinary power and biopower are the modern forms of power to be distinguished from sovereign power. Where sovereign power wholly invests civil society with its political power of decision-making, disciplinary power and the scientific and techno-managerialism of biopower embrace "freedom" at the micro-political level.

The difference between disciplinary power and biopower resides in the way in which the former focuses on the population as masses rather than on the body as a biological unit or on human beings as a species. According to Foucault, liberalism is the framework of biopolitics: the principle of the self-limitation of governmental reason. Liberalism celebrates limited government, governing less, and the maximizing of economic efficiency by putting the individual to work with relative autonomy, and it does so in spite of any political structure that might limit its own self-governance. One might speculate that the relative autonomy today of the social practices that comprise the social formation as a whole extends to individuals themselves: for each individual, a distinct practice; and, furthermore—and crucially—each individual *as* a distinct practice.

But where does this leave the state philosophy of *Juche*? It is my contention, and in these limited remarks I have attempted to sketch out this thesis, that such a philosophy might be broadly compatible with the North Korean "art" of self-governing and the formation of self-reliant subjects endowed with the "free will" to support the dear respected leader. It should go without saying that the state form and the drive toward modernization is a near-universal political ambition and has become a condition of the political. All politics, whether radical or reactionary, must sooner or later "encounter" the liberal nation-state, whether in the form of friend or enemy. But the ongoing and stubborn contradiction of North Korea resides in the fact that its grotesque incarnation of the state form would seem untroubled by and, indeed, in certain key respects perfectly in tune with, the liberal incarnation. Accompanying the driving force and ideology of modernization there is the seeming paradox of an enduring charismatic leadership which revives and perhaps even outdoes the most blatant excesses of Stalin's cult of personality. For this reason, North Korea does not represent an alien form of humanity, having instead come to symbolize one of modernity's monsters: the dangerous outlier of a liberal system where the freedom of self-governance on one hand and more overtly disciplinary forms of government and state repression on the other are differences of degree rather than qualitative differences in kind. Rethinking North Korea from this vantage point will arguably provide a more constructive basis for tackling the far more difficult question of a transition to new and more progressive political regimes.

13.

On the Return
of *Top Gun*

TOP GUN: MAVERICK EXHIBITS how the culture industry shapes the world. The film is not merely a Hollywood blockbuster but a symptomatic revelation of geopolitical reality. The arrival of this sequel to the original *Top Gun* (1986) is timed perfectly for the present moment, when the historical spirit of the earlier film is ripe for recall by Generation X, a cohort reared on 1980s pop culture. Not surprisingly, the nostalgic appeal of the film depends on a specific audience—"Gen Xers." It might be paradoxical that Reaganism has subsisted beyond the rise of Trumpism, a doctrine that implies, to some extent, revenge for the effects of Reaganomics. Those who came of age under the neoliberal Reagan regime in the final years of the Cold War have come a long way through the so-called new world order of the post-Cold War era.

This period since the collapse of the Soviet bloc is sometimes referred to as a thirty-year peace, even though it saw many "low-intensity conflicts." The relatively amicable stability of international relations meant a decline in open conflict between nation-states; contests were mostly confined to civil war and intranational disputes. Yet economic interests rather than political strategy shifted the axis of state violence. Globalization, which brought forth "Global Value Chains" and accelerated the development of universal technology, has changed ways of life across the world. In this global transformation, the United States put its exceptionalism aside and served as an imperial power to sustain the geopolitical balance. The maintenance of Pax Americana was due not only to military action but also to cultural influence on local *modus vivendi*. The latter could be considered the establishment of a master signifier by which the axiomatics of global capitalism are sustained.

After the end of the Eastern Bloc, the United States was perceived as a "soft power" in the geopolitical sense. The new idea of unipolar leadership influenced the understanding of US foreign policy in the post-Cold War era. Few terms have changed the perspective of the US more profoundly than the concept of soft power, which was coined by Joseph Nye in his book *Bound to Lead*. According to Nye, soft power means "getting others to want what you want" through cooperative power resources such as cultural commodities, ideology, and international organizations.[1] However, US soft power only works in combination with hard military dominance over other countries. *Top Gun* portrays both: the soft power of the American culture industry—film, in particular—and a heroic image of American hard power in action.

The economic shocks of the 1970s precipitated the end of the Cold War and the rise of neoliberalism by imposing capitalist interests on labor. The arrival of the 1980s was nothing more than the imposition of economic discipline onto political ideals such as liberal internationalism and communism. Margaret Thatcher's adoption of TINA ("there is no alternative"), a slogan inspired by Herbert Spencer's social evolutionism, urged the imperative of the new world order. Hollywood responded to this ideological transformation, and its aesthetic sentiment became embedded in the axiomatic (re)production of the neoliberal self. The cultural logic of neoliberalism obscured all markers of contemporaneity and gave rise to the illusion of a golden age in the past. Fredric Jameson defined this regressive invention of the past as "nostalgia for the present."

In this way, is it possible to call the 1986 film an exercise in nostalgia in which the history of aesthetic styles displaces real history? Not surprisingly, the belated sequel is retroactively obsessed with its primary scene. What kind of past does this nostalgia imagine? Both films whitewash the concrete experiences of actual wars by focusing on the personal trials and successes of the individual. Interestingly, the original *Top Gun* anticipated the Gulf War, which would occur in 1990, and revealed the ideological fantasy propelling it. Americans got what they desired. There was already a space in the collective imagination reserved for the arrival of the war before it actually happened.

In this "soft" Hollywood fantasy, failed military action involving the confirmed facts of actual wars is romanticized, and the traumatic experiences of a shameful history disappear in the fictitious story of charismatic heroes. In these films, even the enemy aircraft were entirely fake: the planes called "MiG-28s" in the original *Top Gun* did not exist, and the details of Russia's Sukhoi Su-57 in the sequel were not mentioned. Some critics affirmed that *Top Gun* helped the United States forget the painful experiences of the Vietnam War and bolstered American nationalism. If the neoliberal self-help story relied on the logic of nostalgia, what was its sentimental recollection longing for? The pledge of Reagan's 1980 campaign (revived by Trump in 2016) was to "Make America Great Again." Here, the emphasis of the slogan is not "great" but "again"—America must be great AGAIN! This unrestrained call for repetition marks the hidden excess behind the return of *Top Gun*.

If you want to make America great again, two things naturally follow: that America was at one time great and that the country is no longer great today. Nostalgia is rooted in the sense that something of value has been lost. In a Freudian sense, nostalgia is the memory of memories; its emotional mechanism is permanently distorted by an invented impression of the past. The sense of nostalgia rests on symbols, but its object is not equivalent to any original object. The displacement of nostalgic feelings aims at saving the object, and its guilty pleasure is mixed with an aggression toward the original object or, rather, toward the nonexistence of this object.

Top Gun is a symbolic fiction that aims to save America's original "greatness" in the past rather than achieve a great America in the future. In the sequel, this hidden impetus implements a paradoxical setting in which human pilots must prove their usefulness in the age of drone warfare by risking their lives through useless dogfights. Here, the idealization of dogfights serves as the archetype of free (or just) competition. Even the original story draws from an archetype that dates back more than a century. H. G. Wells was the first storyteller to create the early ideal of dogfights in his 1899 dystopian science fiction novel *When the Sleeper Wakes*; the idea of the heroic pilot in air combat was born before the airplane had even been invented:

> Throb, throb, throb—throb, throb, throb; up he drove. He fancied himself free of all excitement, felt cool and deliberate. He lifted the stem still more, opened one valve on his left wing and swept round and up. He looked down with a steady head, and up. One of the Ostrogite monoplanes was driving across his course, so that he drove obliquely towards it and would pass below it at a steep angle. Its little aeronauts were peering down at him. What did they mean to do? His mind became active. One, he saw, held a weapon pointing, seemed prepared to fire. What did they think he meant to do? Instantly he understood their tactics, and his resolution was taken. His momentary lethargy was past. He opened two more valves to his left, swung round, end on to this hostile machine, closed his valves, and shot straight at it, stem and windscreen shielding him from the shot. They tilted a little as if to clear him. He flung up his stem.
>
> Throb, throb, throb—pause—throb, throb— he set his teeth, his face into an involuntary grimace,

and crash! He struck it! He struck upward beneath the nearer wing.[2]

This unconscious level of airborne warfare is the groundless ground of the melancholic nostalgia in the two films. Its symbol formation is supposed to save the original object (i.e., elite Top Gun fighter pilots in a classical sense) for the bygone greatness of America. Reagan's catchphrase manifested a demand for repeating the enjoyment of "Great America," which was believed to be something already lost. If you want to enjoy it, first you must create it. So then, what kind of Great America must be remade by the pseudohistorical epic? In the yacht scene in *Top Gun: Maverick*, the secret clue is disclosed when Pete (Tom Cruise) says, "I don't sail boats, Penny. I land on them." Pete is in the navy but, as a pilot, does not know how to steer a boat. This irony of Pete's existential status tacitly unveils the material condition of "America the Great"—the United States Navy, the world's largest and most powerful navy, which has the world's largest aircraft carrier fleet.

The US Navy became the mightiest navy in the world during World War II by playing a central role in defeating the Japanese empire. After the war, the United States took over the Pacific Ocean and expanded into territories it still occupies to this day. The primary scene of Great America is fabricated by the historical moment of Asia-Pacific geopolitics after World War II, which dramatically replaced the Japanese promise of the Greater East Asia Co-Prosperity Sphere. The original object of *Top Gun*'s nostalgia is nothing other than the American Empire that emerged on the first day of the new Asia-Pacific era. Even though the film lavishly displays the fresh charm of American values and ethics, it is undeniable that *Top Gun: Maverick* is the return of the repressed. In actual history, the US Navy was involved in "the colossal slaughter of the innocents" by deploying atomic bombs during World War II.[3] From this perspective, it is easy to say that the depoliticization of warfare in the films is not an accident but an act of aesthetic complicity in sanitizing America's history. The American dream to repeat greatness continues to wait for another *Top Gun*, and the culture industry is, by now, part of the nightmare.

However, another layer of nostalgia in the new film points to an ideological rupture between the original and its sequel. The follow-up to the 1986 *Top Gun* is, above all, about the legendary character of Pete Mitchell as a "maverick" (his call sign). On the one hand, the film shows us the success of an impossible mission led by Pete; on the other, its reflection on Pete's life betrays the failure of the neoliberal nonconformist. From the start we are told that his is a dying breed: "The future is coming, and you're not in it." *Top Gun: Maverick* does not long for the return of the 1980s. Its sentiment is more inclined toward mourning the end of those years, the death of the neoliberal dream. Its nostalgia has turned into a crisis of melancholia that has no object anymore.

Postscript
View of Delft

A decade ago, I visited Delft, a small Dutch town well-known as the place where the famous painter Johannes Vermeer was born and spent his entire life. The purpose of my trip was to look at Vermeer's painting, *View of Delft*. In those days, I was writing on the Impressionists, and I hinted that the technique Vermeer employed for the work seemed to anticipate Pointillism.

Standing in front of his work, which testified to the Dutch Golden Age, it occurred to me that Vermeer's picture did not show the neighborhood of Delft. Its title indicates that the image is of Delft, but it does not depict any street or interiority of the town or any features of the location, only its façade. It's merely a landscape, and it's quite a monotonous representation. Undoubtedly this was Vermeer's style. However, you could easily watch the everyday life of the town, the vivid reality, even if calm and contemplative, as in other paintings by Vermeer. The representation of daily life, the veneer hiding the natural law or the circle of life, was the typical subject matter of the Northern Renaissance. His aesthetics lay in the revelation of caesura; the rupture of daily temporality. However, *View of Delft* inspired me from a different viewpoint; it was not what I had known of Vermeer up until that time.

I was curious about the setting Vermeer had used for the scene in the painting and decided to look for it. Dutch painters were not as interested in working outdoors as the Impressionists were, and it was not until the nineteenth century that they began bringing their brushes and palettes to the countryside. The traditional painters usually finished the artistic process within their studios. This suggests that rather than having an objective vantage point for the painting, Vermeer may have only had an imagined place within his mind. Nonetheless, I chose my direction and started to step on toward the unknown point.

The problem I faced was that the Dutch people I met did not care about an obsessive enthusiast in search of the imagined place that inspired a painting in a museum. There was no information designating where to go if you want to see the actual location in which Vermeer projected his idea onto the landscape. I traveled all over the place. I have not a brain like an elephant but a sharp nose like a dog in the pose of the pointer. I realized that Delft still had a church that Vermeer had described; finally, I found where the painting was done. There was a small bank covered with clumsy cement. It was not a challenge to square the viewpoint with what Vermeer depicted on his canvas. The pier seemed to still be in use. Small boats and ships were busy shuttling cargo.

That was the moment when an idea occurred to me. What Vermeer accurately represented in his work was nothing less than the very gaze of the outsider, who had just arrived at the outskirts of Delft, a city famous in those days for its trade throughout the world. What is the meaning of the gaze? The gaze belongs to the other, the representation of a total stranger. The purpose of the painting is very intriguing because Vermeer depicted his hometown from the perspective of the foreigner, whose origin was unknown to the people living in Delft. Why did Vermeer take this view of his hometown? Of course, it was a nice place to see the entire landscape of Delft. As a famed painter, he necessarily chose the perfect point to describe the characteristics of the prosperous city. However, his pursuit had further implications.

What was revealed in *View of Delft* was how Vermeer had become estranged from his experiences in the city in which he was born and had grown up. Perhaps he would meet some travelers or traders from different countries, or military officers who had explored the unknown world. Like his contemporaries, Vermeer might listen to what visitors talked about and collect news from them. In *View of Delft*, he discovered a cavity in which the outsider's gaze of alterity should be placed. The gaze was not attributable to any specific person but was instead purely abstract, while the way we see the city was shaped by Vermeer's artistic exercise. Yes, it was an image, or an "image-work" as such. Vermeer sought to establish an objective eye in his depictions of Dutch civil society by endorsing the scientific knowledge of things.

In Vermeer's time, Dutch society transformed from a militaristic state to a civil state, from monarchism to republicanism, and from Catholicism to Calvinism. Above all, the turbulent war ended and was replaced with trade in the market. His paintings indexed the social transition and served as a defender of the new pleasure principle of civil society. *View of Delft* was a by-product of the historical change, the imaginary crystallization of the aesthetic demands in the public sphere. In short, the "image work" embedded in the painting was the representation of modernity, the theorization of the relations between the community and the sovereign power through which the idea of equality came to exist. For Vermeer, the stranger's gaze was the point where the entire scope of the city could be visible. The gaze is mutual. It is not only the other who gazes at me but also I who gaze at them from a different world. In this sense, the outsider's position is the neutral point of conversation, the symbolic exchange of individual interests.

In his painting, Vermeer simply visualized how an image works as a theoretical moment. The gaze of the outsider is the locus of theory. Theory preserves the way to see, a perspective to classify the order of things, which emerges in terms of modernization. Modernity would be the theorization of worldly relations such as community and immunity, interiority and exteriority, politics and economy, etc. The crucial factor in such theorization is the new foundation with which to accredit the new epistemological-aesthetic regime—"I think, therefore I am." This announcement by Descartes would be the new starting point from which the origin of modern subjectivity recognized itself. Vermeer also observed what that subjectivity accounted for. Descartes aspired to achieve a new beginning for the truth by eliminating all preconceptions of knowledge. What he persisted in was a simple argument: one should doubt all received knowledge. Finally, as is well-known, nothing is left except "I think" in epistemology.

Strictly speaking, Descartes's conceptualization of thinking was a way of doubting. So, the proper translation of the original sentence would be "I doubt, therefore I am." To sum up, doubt was the foundation of modern subjectivity, the preparation for rationality. Impressively, his idea was inspired by architectonic imagination. It seems that Descartes's invention of "I think" was indebted to architecture. He adopted a bird's-eye view when recounting the method by which he discovered the absolute foundation of knowledge. From a distance above the earth, a philosopher or an architect can map out the entire scope of the world. This was the moment when the idea of objectivity came to stand for itself. Yes, any idea stands alone once accomplished. There should be self-fulfillment and separation from the generic process. The objectivity is completed as if it has no origin. It contains the origin and the outsider's gaze and finally seals it within itself. What is the origin of objectivity? It might be the real that is missing in the construction of the objectivity, like an architect's gaze when beginning any architectural work.

Vermeer's painting disclosed the secret of the gaze, that is to say, that which objectivity hides within it, the excluded locus of the nameless stranger. He constructed an image of Delft, but its truth came from outside. This structure shows how an image works, not in its content but in its form. The form of a picture reveals the world's reality in this way. Vermeer seemed to understand it and represented a glimpse of the early modern world. In

Vermeer's painting, the stranger's gaze was nothing other than capitalism in Asia, which the Dutch East India Company brought about. The city view of Delft showed the place where the most remote world came directly to Vermeer's feet. Delft was one of six towns in the Netherlands that had a VOC *Kamer* (chamber). In this way, *View of Delft* was the evidence of the capitalist object. The origin of my interest in Asia dates back to when I encountered the painting. The stranger who Vermeer discovered was "Asia," which was reborn with the arrival of the VOC. Capitalism in Asia is the world that it made.

Endnotes

Introduction

1 Quoted in Donald F. Lach, "Leibniz and China," *Journal of the History of Ideas*, 6. no. 4 (October 1945), p. 436.
2 Ibid.
3 Voltaire, "On Smallpox Inoculation," in *Philosophical Letters: Or, Letters Regarding the English Nation*, ed. John Leigh, trans. Prudence L. Steiner (Indianapolis: Hackett, 2007), pp. 35–36.
4 G. W. Leibniz, "Letter to Samuel Masson," in *Philosophical Essays*, trans. Roger Ariew and Daniel Garber (Indianapolis: Hackett, 1989), p. 227.
5 Ibid.
6 Ibid.
7 G.W. Leibniz, "From the Letters to Arnauld," in *Philosophical Essays*, trans. Roger Ariew and Daniel Garber (Indianapolis: Hackett, 1989), p. 89.
8 Ibid.
9 Ibid.
10 Graham Harman, *Immaterialism: Objects and Social Theory* (Cambridge: Polity, 2016), pp. 114–115.
11 Ibid.
12 Kakuzo Okakura, *The Ideals of the East: With Special Reference to the Art of Japan* (San Diego: Stone Bridge Press, 2007), p. 9.
13 Ibid.
14 See Wang Hui, *The Rise of Modern Chinese Thought* (現代中國思想的興起), 4 volumes (Beijing: SDX Joint Publishing Company, 2015).
15 Eric Hobsbawm, *The Age of Extremes: The Short Twentieth Century 1914–1991* (London: Abacus, 1994), p. 226.

16 Fukuzawa Yukichi, "On Leaving Asia" (脱亜論), *Education About Asia,* vol 21:1 (2016), p. 66.
17 Fukuzawa Yukichi, *An Outline of a Theory of Civilization*, trans. David A. Dilworth and G. Cameron Hurst III (New York: Columbia University Press, 2009), p. 48
18 Fukuzawa, "On Leaving Asia," p. 67.
19 Ibid.
20 Marius B. Jansen, *The Japanese and Sun Yat-Sen* (Cambridge, MA: Harvard University Press, 1967), p. 43.
21 Nicole CuUnjieng Aboitiz, *Asian Place, Filipino Nation: A Global Intellectual History of the Philippine Revolution, 1887–1912* (New York: Columbia University Press, 2020), p. 26.
22 Paul Valéry, "The Crisis of the Mind," *An Anthology*, ed. James R. Lawler (London: Routledge, 1977), p. 95.
23 Oswald Spengler, *Man and Technics: A Contribution to a Philosophy of Life*, trans. Charles Francis Atkinson (London: George Allen & Unwin LTD, 1932), p. 101.
24 Ibid., p. 103.

Chapter One

1 Zygmunt Bauman, *Globalization: The Human Consequences* (Oxford: Polity Press, 1998), pp. 55–56.
2 Slavoj Žižek, *The Sublime Object of Ideology* (London: Verso, 1989), pp. 9–10.
3 Howard Nicholas, *Marx's Theory of Price and its Modern Rivals* (London: Palgrave, 2011), p. 7.
4 Karl Marx, *Capital: A Critique of Political Economy*, vol. 3, trans. David Fernbach (London: Penguin, 1981), p. 288.
5 Ibid.
6 Karl Marx and Friedrich Engels, *Marx-Engels Collected Works*, vol. 24 (London: Lawrence and Wishart, 2010), p. 448.
7 Karl Marx, *Capital: A Critique of Political Economy*, vol. 1, trans. Ben Fawkes (London: Penguin, 1976), p. 178.
8 Evgeny Pashukanis, *Law and Marxism: A General Theory*, trans. Barbara Einhorn (London: Pluto, 1989), p. 110.

9   Ibid., p. 113.
10 Pierre Dardot and Christian Laval, *The New Way of the World: On Neoliberal Society*, trans. Gregory Elliott (London: Verso, 2013), p. 39.
11 Karl Marx, *A Contribution to the Critique of Political Economy* (New York: International Publishers, 1970), p. 21.
12 Marx and Engels, *Marx-Engels Collected Works*, vol. 24, p. 364.

Chapter Two

1   Karl Marx, *Capital: A Critique of Political Economy*, vol. 1, trans. Ben Fawkes (London: Penguin, 1990), p. 915.
2   Deborah Cowen, *The Deadly Life of Logistics: Mapping Violence in Global Trade* (Minneapolis: The University of Minnesota Press, 2014), pp. 8–9.
3   Thomas Hobbes, *Leviathan* (Indianapolis: Hackett, 1994), p. 104.
4   Michel Foucault, *The Punitive Society: Lectures at the Collège de France 1972–1973*, trans. Graham Burchell (London: Palgrave, 2015), p. 24.
5   Ibid., pp. 25–26.
6   Ibid., p. 26.
7   Jan Nederveen Pieterse, *Globalization and Culture: Global Mélange* (London: Rowman and Littlefield, 2009), p. 71.
8   Marc Augé, *Non-Places: Introduction to an Anthropology of Supermodernity*, trans. John Howe (London: Verso, 1995), pp. 77–78.
9   Ibid., p. 74.
10 Ibid., p. 40.
11 Karl Marx and Frederick Engels, *The Communist Manifesto* (New York: International Publishers, 1948), p. 12.
12 Dean MacCannell, *The Tourist: A New Theory of the Leisure Class* (Berkeley: The University of California Press, 2013), p. 100.
13 Daniel J. Boorstin, *The Image: A Guide to Pseudo-Events in America* (New York: Vintage, 1987), p. 91.
14 MacCannell, *Tourist.*, p. 102.
15 Ibid., p. 62.

16 Hiroki Azuma, *The Philosophy of the Tourist* 観光客の哲学 (Tokyo: Genron, 2017), p. 157.
17 Antonio Negri and Michael Hardt, *Empire* (Cambridge, MA: Harvard University Press, 2000), p. 15.
18 Azuma, *Philosophy of the Tourist*, p. 146.
19 Negri and Hardt, *Empire*, p. 413.
20 Ibid., p. 411.
21 Antonio Negri and Michael Hardt, *Multitude: War and Democracy in the Age of Empire* (London: Penguin, 2004), p. 192.
22 Ibid., p. 105.
23 Gilles Deleuze and Félix Guattari, *Anti-Oedipus: Capitalism and Schizophrenia*, trans. Robert Hurley, Mark Seem and Helen R. Lane (Minneapolis: University of Minnesota Press, 1983), p. 237.
24 Azuma, *Philosophy of the Tourist*, p. 192.
25 Karl Marx, *Grundrisse: Foundations of the Critique of Political Economy*, trans. Martin Nicolaus (London: Penguin, 1993), p. 92.
26 Ibid., p. 202.

Chapter Three

1 Qun Li et al., "Early Transmission Dynamics in Wuhan, China, of Novel Coronavirus–Infected Pneumonia," *The New England Journal of Medicine*, 382, no. 13. 2020.
2 Shengjie Lai et al., "Effect of non-pharmaceutical interventions for containing the COVID-19 outbreak in China," MedRxiv.org. https://www.medrxiv.org/content/10.1101/2020.03.03.20029843v3.full.pdf
3 See "Why Wuhan is so important to China's economy and the potential impact of the coronavirus," January 24, 2020. *South China Morning Post*. https://www.scmp.com/economy/china-economy/article/3047426/explained-why-wuhan-so-important-chinas-economy-and-potential
4 Slavoj Žižek, "Coronavirus is 'Kill Bill'-esque blow to capitalism and could lead to reinvention of communism," February 27, 2020. https://www.rt.com/op-ed/481831-coronavirus-kill-bill-capitalism-communism/

5   Slavoj Žižek, "Communism or babarism, it's that simple," An interview with Renata Ávila, DiEM25 TV. https://dialektika.org/en/2020/04/01/slavoj-zizek-on-coronavirus-communism-or-barbarism-that-simple-video/
6   Byung-Chul Han, "La emergencia viral y el mundo de mañana," March 23, 2020, *El País*. https://elpais.com/ideas/2020-03-21/la-emergencia-viral-y-el-mundo-de-manana-byung-chul-han-el-filosofo-surcoreano-que-piensa-desde-berlin.html
7   Roberto Esposito, "Biopolitics and Coronavirus: A View from Italy," March 31, 2020, *The Philosophical Salon*. http://thephilosophicalsalon.com/biopolitics-and-coronavirus-a-view-from-italy/
8   Susan Watkins, "The Political State of the Union," *New Left Review* 90 (2014), pp. 5–6.

Chapter Four

1   Marx, *Capital*, vol. 1., p. 343.
2   Toby Shorin, "Haute Baroque Capitalism," *Subpixel Space*, April 11, 2017. https://subpixel.space/entries/haute-baroque-capitalism/
3   Flavio Pintarelli, "Louis Vuitton, Baroque Capitalism and the End of the World," *Domus*. July 4, 2019. https://www.domusweb.it/en/opinion/2019/07/03/louis-vuitton-baroque-capitalism-and-the-end-of-the-world.html
4   Marx, *Capital*, vol.1., p. 344.
5   Gilles Deleuze and Félix Guattari, *A Thousand Plateaus: Capitalism and Schizophrenia II*, trans. Brian Massumi (Minneapolis: University of Minnesota Press, 1987), p. 447.
6   Ibid.

Chapter Five

1   Immanuel Kant, *Towards Perpetual Peace and Other Writings*, trans. David L. Colclasure (New Haven: Yale University Press, 2006), p. 82.
2   Ibid.

3   See John C. Torpey, *The Invention of the Passport: Surveillance, Citizenship and the State* (Cambridge: Cambridge University Press, 2018), pp. 143–144.
4   Hannah Arendt, *The Origins of Totalitarianism* (New York: Harcourt, 1973), p. 267.
5   Gavin Walker, "Nationalism and the National Question," in *The SAGE Handbook of Marxism* (London: SAGE, 2022), p. 377.
6   Marx, *Capital*, vol. 1., p. 178.
7   Walker, "Nationalism and the National Question," p. 372.
8   Étienne Balibar and Immanuel Wallerstein, *Race, Nation, Class: Ambiguous Identities* (New York: Verso, 1991), p. 86.
9   Ibid., p. 93.
10 Ibid., p. 86.
11 Karl Marx, *A Contribution to the Critique of Political Economy*, trans. N. I. Stone (Chicago: Charles H. Kerr and Company, 1904), pp. 265–266.
12 Ibid.
13 Ibid., p. 268.
14 Ibid., p. 269.
15 Ibid.
16 Ibid.
17 Ibid., pp. 272–273.
18 Bernard Stiegler, "Automatic society, Londres février 2015," trans. Daniel Ross, *Journal of Visual Art Practice*, 15, Nos. 2–3 (2016), p. 196.
19 Catherine Malabou, "Cryptocurrencies: Anarchist Turn or Strengthening of Surveillance Capitalism? From Bitcoin to Libra," trans. Robert Boncardo, *Australian Humanities Review* 66 (May 2020), p. 146.
20 Jacques Rancière, *The Nights of Labor*, trans. John Drury (Philadephia: Temple University Press, 1989), p. 15.

Chapter Six

1   Jeremy Bentham, *The Panopticon Writings*, ed. Miran Božovič (London: Verso, 1995), p. 34.

2. Byung-Chul Han, "The smartphone is a tool of domination. It acts like a rosary." https://english.elpais.com/usa/2021-10-15/byung-chul-han-the-smartphone-is-a-tool-of-domination-it-acts-like-a-rosary.html
3. Robert Pfaller, *Interpassivity: The Aesthetics of Delegated Enjoyment* (Edinburgh: Edinburgh University Press, 2017), p. 16.

Chapter Seven

1. Jacques Rancière, *The Politics of Aesthetics*, trans. Gabriel Rockhill (London: Continuum, 2004), p. 13.
2. Michel Foucault, *The Birth of Biopolitics: Lectures at the Collège de France, 1978–79*, ed. Michel Senellart, trans. Graham Burchell (London: Palgrave, 2008), p. 20.
3. Ibid., p. 4.
4. Dianna Taylor, ed. *Michel Foucault: Key Concepts* (Durham: Acumen, 2011), p. 54.
5. Matt Stiles, "In South Korea's Hypercompetitive Job Market, It Helps to Be Attractive," *Los Angeles Times*, June 13, 2017. http://www.latimes.com/world/asia/la-fg-south-korea-image-2017-story.html
6. Ibid.
7. Vladimir Tikhonov, *Social Darwinism and Nationalism in Korea: The Beginnings (1880s–1910s): "Survival" as an Ideology of Korean Modernity* (Leiden: Brill, 2010), p. 21.
8. Ibid., pp. 25–26.
9. Hao Chang, *Liang Ch'i-ch'ao and Intellectual Transition in China 1890–1907* (Cambridge, MA: Harvard University Press, 1971), pp. 65–66.

Chapter Eight

1. Naomi Klein, *The Shock Doctrine: The Rise of Disaster Capitalism* (New York: Metropolitan Books, 2007), p. 81.
2. https://news.caijingmobile.com/article/detail/428729?source_id=40

3   G. W. F. Hegel, *The Science of Logic*, trans. George Giovanni (Cambridge: Cambridge University Press, 2010), p. 651.
4   Ibid., p. 630.
5   Ibid.
6   Félix Guattari, "Vers une ère post-média," *Chimères* 1996/2 (N° 28).
7   Ibid., pp. 16–17.
8   Gilles Deleuze, *Difference and Repetition*, trans. Paul Patton (New York: Columbia University Press, 1994), p.222.

Chapter Nine

1   Jacques Rancière, "What Medium Can Mean," *Parrhesia*, trans. Steven Corcoran (November 11, 2011), p. 37.
2   Ibid.
3   Ibid., p. 36.
4   Marx, *Grundrisse*, p. 706.
5   Rancière, "What Medium Can Mean," p. 43.
6   Walter Benjamin, *Selected Writings, vol. 2: 1931–1934*, eds. Michael W. Jennings, Howard Eiland, and Gary Smith (Cambridge, MA: Harvard University Press, 1999), p. 777.
7   Ibid., p. 780.
8   Rancière, "What Medium Can Mean," p. 43

Chapter Ten

1   Yoav Di-Capua, *No Exit: Arab Existentialism, Jean-Paul Sartre, and Decolonization* (Chicago: University of Chicago Press, 2018), p. 2.
2   Rosa Luxemburg, *The National Question: Selected Writings*, ed. Horace B. Davis (New York: Monthly Review Press, 1976), p. 157.
3   Ibid., pp. 159–160.
4   Vladimir Ilyich Lenin, *Collected Works*, vol. 20 (Moscow: Progress Publishers, 1964), p. 422.
5   Hugh De Saint Victor, *The Didascalicon of Hugh of Saint Victor: A Guide to the Arts*, trans. Jerome Taylor (New York: Columbia University Press, 1991), p. 101.

6 Hannah Arendt, *The Origins of Totalitarianism* (New York: Harcourt, 1973), p. 267.

Chapter Eleven

1 Behrooz Ghamari-Tabrizi, *Foucault in Iran: Islamic Revolution after the Enlightenment* (Minneapolis: University of Minnesota Press, 2016), p. 161.
2 Janet Afary and Kevin B. Anderson, *Foucault and the Iranian Revolution: Gender and the Seductions of Islamism* (Chicago: The University of Chicago Press, 2005), p. 255.
3 Ibid.
4 Ibid., p. 254.
5 Ibid., p. 169.
6 Ibid., p. 168.
7 Ghamari-Tabrizi, *Foucault in Iran*, p. 184.
8 Afary and Anderson, *Foucault and the Iranian Revolution*, p. 189.
9 Michel Foucault, *Power: The Essential Works of Foucault, 1954–1984, vol.3*, ed. James D. Faubion, trans. Robert Hurley (New York: The New Press, 2001), p. 233.
10 Ali Shari'ati, *Marxism and Other Western Fallacies: An Islamic Critique*, trans. Robert Campbell (Berkeley: Mizan Press, 1980), p. 95.
11 Ibid., p. 45.
12 See Gilles Deleuze's conversation with Foucault in *L'Arc* 49 (1972), pp. 3–10. Michel Foucault, "Intellectuals and Power," in *Language, Counter-Memory, Practice: Selected Essays and Interviews*, ed. Donald F. Bouchard, trans. Donald F. Bouchard and Sherry Simon (Ithaca: Cornell University Press, 1977), p. 208.
13 Foucault, *The Punitive Society*, pp. 25–26.
14 Carl Schmitt, *Political Theology: Four Chapters on the Concept of Sovereignty*, trans. George Schwab (Chicago: The University of Chicago Press, 1985), p. 10.
15 Ibid., pp. 51–52.
16 Ibid., p. 65.
17 Ibid.
18 Shari'ati, *Marxism and Other Western Fallacies*, p. 120.

19 Michel Foucault, *Foucault Live: Interviews, 1961–1984*, ed. Sylvère Lotringer, trans. Lysa Hochroth and John Johnston (New York: Semiotext(e), 1989), p. 223.
20 Foucault, *Power*, p. 451.
21 Michel Foucault, *The History of Sexuality, vol. 2: The Use of Pleasure*, trans. Robert Hurley (New York: Vintage, 1986), p. 10.

Chapter Twelve

1 Jon Halliday, "The North Korean Enigma," *New Left Review* 127 (1980), p. 18.
2 Mark Millar et al., *Superman: Red Son* (New York: DC Comics, 2004).
3 Bryan Myers, *The Cleanest Race: How North Koreans See Themselves and Why It Matters* (New York Melville House, 2010), p. 30.
4 Chong-Sik Lee and Robert A. Scalapino, *North Korea: Building of the Monolithic State* (Berwyn: The KHU Press, 2017), p. 43.
5 Ibid., p. 83.
6 Carl Schmitt, *The Crisis of Parliamentary Democracy*, trans. Allen Kennedy (Cambridge, MA: The MIT Press, 1988), pp. 14–15.
7 Chantal Mouffe, *The Democratic Paradox* (London: Verso, 2000), p. 43.
8 Kim Il Sung, *Juche!: Speeches and Writings of Kim Il Sung*, ed. Li Yuk-Sa (New York: Grossman Publishers, 1972), p. 117.
9 Ibid.
10 Ibid., p. 118.
11 Joseph Stalin, *Works*, vol. 14 (London: Red Star Press, 1978), p. 320.
12 Kim, *Juche!*, p. 120.
13 Barbara Demick, *Nothing to Envy: Ordinary Lives in North Korea* (New York: Spiegel & Grau, 2010), p. 44.
14 Ibid.
15 Victor Cha, *The Impossible State: North Korea, Past and Future* (New York: Ecco, 2013), p. 7.
16 Ibid., p. 13.

17 Heonik Kwon and Byung-Ho Chung, *North Korea: Beyond Charismatic Politics* (London: Rowan & Littlefield Publishers, 2012), p. 1.
18 Ibid.
19 Max Weber, *The Theory of Social and Economic Organization*, ed. Talcott Parsons, trans. A. M. Henderson and Talcott Parsons (New York: The Free Press, 1947), p. 386.
20 Ibid.
21 Kwon and Chung, *North Korea*, pp. 44–45.
22 Ibid., p. 44.
23 Ibid., p. 45.
24 Myers, *Cleanest Race*, p. 97.
25 Marcus Tullius Cicero, *On Commonwealth and On the Laws*, trans. James Zetzel (Cambridge: Cambridge University Press, 1999), p. 1.
26 Ann-Cathrin Harders, "Beyond *Oikos* and *Domus*: Modern Kinship Studies and the Ancient Family," in *Families in the Greco-Roman World*, eds. Ray Laurence and Agneta Stromberg (London: Continuum, 2012), p.17.
27 Ibid.
28 On the relation between myth and law, see Jean-Pierre Vernant and Pierre Vidal-Naquet, *Myth and Tragedy in Ancient Greece* (New York: Zone Books, 1988).
29 Myers, *Cleanest Race*, p. 37.
30 Ibid.
31 Kim, *Juche!*, p. 30.

Chapter Thirteen

1 Joseph S. Nye Jr., *Bound to Lead: The Changing Nature of American Power* (New York: Basic Books, 1990), 31–32.
2 H. G. Wells, *When the Sleeper Wakes* (Digibooks OOD / Demera Publishing, Bulgaria, 1899), 176.
3 Dorothy Day, "We Go On Record: The CW Response to Hiroshima," *The Catholic Worker* 41, no. 06 (July–August 1975).

www.ingramcontent.com/pod-product-compliance
Lightning Source LLC
Chambersburg PA
CBHW020459030426
42337CB00011B/161